## Identification & Value Guide To

# TEXTILE BAGS

by

Anna Lue Cook

*To*
*Ralph and Tammy*

ISBN 0-89689-080-5

# ACKNOWLEDGEMENTS

The "Bag Lady" would like to take this opportunity to thank all the wonderful people who helped me during my research and preparation of this book.

First, I would like to thank all members of my family who helped me and gave me support and encouragement when I needed it.

Second, I would like to thank the following bag manufacturers for sharing information with me about bag manufacturing and the history of their companies: Bemis Company, Inc.; Central Bag Company; Chase Bag Company; Fulton-Denver Company; Hutchinson Bag Corporation; Langston Bags; Percy Kent Bag Company, Inc; Semmes Bag Company; and Werthan Industries, Incorporated.

A very special thank you to my friend, Laura Mize, who took the time to share information with me about the textile bags and their manufacture.

My deep appreciation goes to the following museums, business firms and individuals that took their time to share information and items with me: American Textile Manufacturers Institute; Russell Carpenter; Monnie Cook; Herbert Hoover Library, West Branch, Iowa; I. J. Hurdle Gin and Laurel Hurdle; Museum of American Textile History; National Cotton Council; National Museum of American History, Rita Adrosko, Curator for the Division of Textiles; and Merikay Woldvogel.

Last, I would like to say thank you to all the antique shops, flea market vendors, antique appraisers, auctioneers, auction houses, fellow sack collectors and individuals across our nation that took the time to write to me, talk with me and share information about the textile bags.

My love of the textile bags spans most of my lifetime. I hope this book inspires others to enjoy the textile bags as much as I do.

# TABLE OF CONTENTS

# INTRODUCTION

Textiles is fast becoming an important area of collecting. Within this area, the cotton textile bags that packaged everything from flour to feed is attracting interest in the antique field and with museums as well. The textile bag that began as a plain white bag for packaging food staples in the last half of the nineteenth century developed into one of the hottest advertised and promoted items of the twentieth century. During this time, the textile bag became the single most popular way of clothing the American family as well as decorating the home. These bags were recycled by the American housewife in every way from making underwear for family members to making curtains and dish towels for the home.

These textile bags documented the pages of our past. They tell of the products that America purchased and the emblems and pictures printed on these bags give a pictorial narrative of rural America.

The pricing of the textile bags is a new area and one where there is no past prices to rely on. Therefore, the pricing was difficult. Most antique guides don't even list the lowly textile bag and the ones that do give prices ranging from $5 to $500. The prices in this guide are based on what the cotton textile bags are selling for across the U.S.A. in antique shops, malls, flea markets and auctions. Also considered, was the fact that some sizes of the textile bags are rare and naturally those have a higher value.

Many individuals across our nation can remember wearing feed sack clothes when they were children. Girls were dressed in starched, ruffled feed sack dresses. Boys wore feed sack shirts. Many items for the house such as towels, sheets, quilts and curtains made from the cotton textile bags are hard to find because they were made for everyday wearing and they were used up, worn out and thrown away. From out of the past, we can still catch colorful glimpses of the cotton textile bags. These may appear from the everyday flea market to the most sophisticated museums. The following poem is by an unknown author but it tells about the reality of having to use the cotton textile bags.

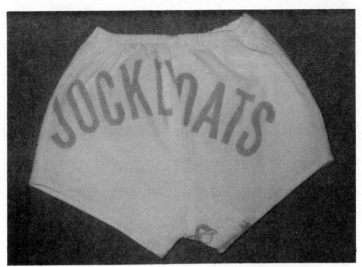

## DEPRESSION FLOUR-SACK UNDERWEAR

When I was just a maiden fair,
Mama made our underwear;
With many kids and Dad's poor pay,
We had no fancy lingerie.
Monograms and fancy stitches
Did not adorn our Sunday britches;
Pantywaists that stood the test
Had "Swans Down" on my breast.
No lace or ruffles to Enhance,
Just "Jockey Oats" on my pants.
One pair of Panties beat them all,
For it had a scene I still recall –
Chickens were eating wheat
Right across my little seat.
Rougher than a grizzly bear
Was my flour-sack underwear,
Plain, not fancy and two feet wide
And tougher than a hippo's hide.
All through Depression each Jill and Jack
Wore the sturdy garb of sack.
Waste not, want not, we soon learned
That a penny saved is a penny earned.
There were curtains and tea towels, too,
And that is just to name a few,
But the best beyond compare
Was my flour-sack underwear.

# CHAPTER 1

## HISTORY OF THE TEXTILE BAG

Cotton fields across the wide expanse of America's farmland produced a product that revolutionized the packaging business in the last half of the nineteenth century and the first half of the twentieth century. The cotton textile bag for packaging food staples such as flour, sugar, meal, salt and feed began replacing the wooden barrels and kegs around the middle of the 1800's. For about the first two hundred years of early life in America, the only containers for food products were the wooden barrel, keg, box or tin. It is not certain when the first textile bag was used in the United States, but sometime in the first half of the nineteenth century. These first textile bags would have been homespun, hand sewn and expensive to use. They did not gain favor with manufacturers until several years later. From this lowly beginning, the cotton textile bag would reach its peak of popularity some one hundred years later.

The flour manufacturers were the largest industry to use the barrel for shipping their product. Later they would be the largest user of the cotton textile bags. At the time the textile bag was first introduced, about one hundred and fifty years ago, it was expensive to use and did not become popular with manufacturers. Individuals, at this time, used the hand made cotton textile bags to carry their wheat and corn to the gristmills to be ground into flour and meal. They could throw a bag over the back of a horse easier than they could throw a wooden barrel over the back of that horse.

During the years 1820 through 1840, the bag stamp mold was used by farmers. They carved these wooden blocks with their names or initials on them. The farmers would stamp their bags so the miller would know who the grain belonged to. Sometimes interesting patterns like flowers, wheat or hearts were added to the mold.

Elias Howe developed the sewing machine in 1846 and at this time, manufacturers began to develop a sewing machine to sew the cotton textile bags with. According to Dr. Terry Sharrer of the Division of Agriculture and Natural Resources at the National Museum of American History, J.M Hurd of Auburn, NY patented a flour sack machine in August 1864. Both of these inventions increased the use of the textile bag, but the wooden barrel was still the most popular way to package through the 1880's. The textile bags began to grow in popularity from 1880 on and before the beginning of the 1900's, it was more popular than the barrel. By the time of the first World War, the barrel was almost nonexistent.

According to the Herbert Hoover Presidential Library at West Branch, Iowa, during World War I, the Commission for Relief in Belgium shipped almost 700,000,000 pounds of flour into Belgium to help feed the people there. All this flour was shipped in cotton textile bags. These textile cotton sacks were carefully accounted for and distributed to professional schools, convents and sewing workrooms. They used the flour sacks in particular to make new clothing, accessories, pillows, bags, etc. Many of these sacks were selected for the purpose of doing embroidery work over the mill logo and the relief flour brand names. Many times new designs were embroidered or painted on the sacks.

The completed flour sacks were sold through shops in Belgium, England and America for the purpose of raising funds for various relief organizations. Many of these works of art were given as gifts to the Commission for Relief in Belgium in gratitude for their help to the Belgian people. Several of these sacks are on display at the Herbert Hoover Presidential Library at West Branch, Iowa.

Evidence indicates that sugar and grains were also shipped to Belgium as part of the relief effort.

This picture, courtesy of the Herbert Hoover Libarary, West Branch, IA, shows sacks of flour ready for shipment to Belgium during World War I.

This picture shows one of the decorated flour bags done by the Belgium people. This picture is courtesy of the Herbert Hoover Library, West Branch, IA.

The early hand sewn textile bags were over-and-over handsewn bags and were considered stronger until the machine sewn bags were proven. Once proven and accepted by the milling industry, the packaging business converted from the barrel to the textile bags. Barrels of flour weighed 196 pounds. Because the flour industry would be the largest user of the textile bags, the weights of the bags corresponded to the weight of the flour barrel at the beginning of the conversion from barrels to bags. A barrel size bag would weigh 196 pounds, one half barrel bags would weigh 98 pounds; 49 or 48 pound bags were equivalent to the one-fourth barrel; the one-eighth barrel bag would weigh 24 to 24½ pounds; and a bag that weighed 12 or 12¼ pounds was equivalent to one sixteenth of a barrel. A 12¼ pound bag of flour sold for 40¢ in 1909 and by 1911 it was selling for 45¢.

While the textile bag was developing and becoming "the way" to package products, many sizes of bags were used other than the ones mentioned above. By 1914, the housewife started to demand more sanitized ways of packaging than the bulk provided. This was when the smaller textile bag began to become popular. Textile bags with measurements like 49, 48, 24, 12 6, 4, 3 and 2 pounds became popular. The textile bags ranged in size from the small 1 pounder to the large cotton pick sack that was 9 to 12 feet long and used to pick cotton.

The following pictures show textile bags in the one-half barrel, the one-fourth barrel, the one-eighth barrel, and the one-sixteenth barrel size bags.

This 98 pound BIRCHMONT flour bag is a one-half barrel size bag. The bag measures 35x20 inches.

This 48 pound bag is a one-fourth barrel size bag. The SWANS DOWN flour bag measures 29x15 inches.

This 24 pound LADY CLAIR flour bag is a one-eighth barrel size. It measures 25½x12 inches.

This 12 pound ASCENSION flour bag is a one-sixteenth barrel size. The bag measures 17½x11 inches.

There were no certain set measurements for the textile bags until the War Production Board ordered a standard measurement in 1943 of six sizes – 100, 50, 25, 10, 5 and 2 pound sizes. At that time, most manufacturers converted to these six basic sizes for their products. These basic measurements are still much in use today with the exception of cement. Cement is still sold in bag sizes to correspond with the barrel measurements. A barrel of cement weighs 376 pounds. A bag of cement is usually sold in the ¼ barrel size or 94 pound bags.

During the depression years, cotton bags came into ever increasing demand because the housewife could reuse the bags and stretch the hard to come by pennies. The first early manufactured bags were in solid cottons in white, browns and sometimes colors. Sometime during the 1920's or early 1930's, the bag manufacturers began to make the figured or dress print textile bags. These became very popular with the lady of the house because of the reuse value. The textile cotton bag, white, colored and print, reached its peak of popularity during the 1930's, 1940's and 1950's. During 1942, about 50,000,000 print flour and feed bags were manufactured and sold.

Most of those were recycled by the American housewife. These print bags were truly a part of every rural American home during the 1930's and 1940's. In March 1942, it was estimated that 3,000,000 American farm women and children of all income levels were wearing print feed bag garments. This was true for not only economy but because the materials were so attractive.

According to the Bemis Brother Bag Company, sales and delivery statistics showed that the following eight general classes of bag consuming industries accounted for approximately 90% of Bemis total cotton bag unit sales:

| | |
|---|---|
| Flour | 42.4% |
| Sugar | 17.2% |
| Feed | 11.4% |
| Seeds | 9.7% |
| Rice | 3.8% |
| Corn Meal | 2.8% |
| Meal – all others | 1.8% |
| Fertilizer | .6% |

There are three main kinds of cotton cloth used in cotton bag manufacture, cotton sheetings, print cloths and osnaburgs. The osnaburg is usually an off white made with a cheaper grade of cotton. It is made with coarse yarn, low count and with a rugged strength that makes it good for repeat usage. These osnaburg bags were cheap to make and usually used for grains, seeds, feeds, meals and export flour.

Sheetings are of three grades, class A the heaviest, class B the next heaviest and last is class C. Sheetings are made with a higher thread count than osnaburg is. It is made with a fairly clean white cotton. Sheetings are made for products like sugar, salt and flour that need a strong bag to prevent sifting. It gives a good merchandising appearance.

Print cloth is made from clean white cotton with a higher count of finer yarns than sheetings. Print cloth is usually bleached and printed with dress goods patterns for reuse by the housewife.

After the desired materials had been received, the textile mills began the cutting, folding, sewing, clipping, turning and baling. Depending on the fold and cut, three things can result:

1 – the raw edge appears on the sides with the selvage at the top and bottom;

2 – the selvage appears on the side seam with the raw edges at the top and bottom;

3 – the material could be folded at the bottom with the raw edges at the hem on top. The selvage would be along both sides where there

would be seams as in the cotton picking sacks used years ago. Most feed and flour textile bags were made with the selvage at the top and bottom.

The bags were usually sewn with a double-locked stitch with 11 stitches to two inches which makes a strong seam. The seam could be unraveled simply by unlocking the stitch at the beginning or ending of the seam. After unlocking the stitch, pull the needle and looper threads on each side.

After the bags had been made, they were turned and printed or labeled with company logos and name brands. One way this was done was by direct on the bag printing, mainly on the front. The white textile bags were the ones with printing directly on the bag itself. The ink used for this printing was in a variety of colors and usually an ink that could be washed out so the housewife could reuse the bag. The washout instructions were usually printed on the bags. The two pictures both show the white cotton textile bags with direct on bag printing.

| | |
|---|---|
| The OMEGA flour bag is an excellent example of printing on the white textile bag. It measures 25x12 inches. | This 25 pound bag of RED HEAD corn meal is another excellent example of direct printing on a white textile bag. The bag measures 26x13 inches. |

9

Band-labels were used on some bags instead of direct ink printing. This band labeling was applied on both the print and white bags. The paper labels were sewn into the seam of the bag and could be removed by soaking the bag in water. The bag would then be ready for reuse.

An example of band-labeling on a white cotton textile bag is the 50 pound MILKWHITE flour bag. The bag measures 29½x17 inches.

The 100 pound bag of CORNO feed is an excellent example of the band-labeling. The bag measures 24x22 inches.

10

Spot pasted labels are paper labels which have been printed separately and pasted to the face of the bag. These labels are popular on the print textile bags. The spot label could be removed by soaking the bag in water.

The 10 pound bag of SOUTHERN QUEEN flour is an excellent example of spot labeling. The bag measures 17x10½ inches.

This 25 pound bag of AMERICAN BEAUTY flour is an excellent example of spot labeling. The bag measures 24x12 inches.

After the bags were printed or labeled, they were inspected, baled in convenient bundles of 100, covered with either cotton or burlap and shipped to an industry for use. Most bags manufactured during the 1930's, 1940's and 1950's had washing directions printed either on the bag or on the labels. The bag manufacturers wanted the thrifty housewife to reuse as many of their bags as was possible. Many bag manufacturers used unique ideas to entice the lady of the house to buy their bag and the product that came in it. Some of these ideas were the flour bags that had sewn-in drawstrings; the buyer had only to rip out the one seam and she had a gaily printed cotton apron.

Other manufacturers put outlines for stuffed toys, dolls and children's dresses on the bags. Still others made ready to use flour bag pillowcases.

The lowly feed sack, once referred to as "chicken linen" became so attractive during these years that no one was embarrassed to wear clothes made from the sacks. The phrase "chicken linen" came about because farmers' wives raised chickens to make extra spending money during this time. The feed that they fed the chickens was packaged in the print and white textile bags. The housewife reused the bags in her home. In 1942, one mill was making print bag cloth in 1000 different colorful designs. Many want to forget the hard times of the depression when using the cloth from textile bags was necessary, but the gaily printed bags and items made from them have a definite place in our Americana antique collections.

# CHAPTER 2

## HISTORY OF TEXTILE BAG MANUFACTURERS

Cotton bags were textile products which were rarely, if ever, seen in swank display rooms and which were seldom depicted in slick paper magazines. Agriculture, industry and the home provided an important market for cotton bags and bagging during years past. Many of the early cotton textile bag manufacturers that made these bags began their companies during the mid nineteenth century. Some 130 years later many of those same bag manufacturers are still leaders in the packaging business. The bag industry began with the burlap and cotton textile bags and now the bag-container industry is mainly the plastic bags and the multiwall paper bag. Very few cotton textile bags are currently produced.

Consumption of cotton fabrics in bags climbed from 816 million yards in 1939 to 1,283 million yards in 1946. Bags accounted for about 8.0% of the cotton goods production and 4.5% of total cotton consumption in the U.S. in 1946. According to *Davison's Textile Blue Book* for 1932 there were 24 textile mills manufacturing the bag goods. In 1942, the same volume listed 31 textile mills that manufactured bag goods. In 1952, there were 33 mills listed. The names of some of the mills listed were: Alabama Mills Co., of Birmingham, Ala.; Bemis Brother Bag Co., of St. Louis, Missouri; Fulton Bag and Cotton Mills of Atlanta, Ga.; Royal River Mills of Yarmouth, Me.; Laurel Mills of Laurel, Miss.; Flint River Cotton Mills of Albany, Ga.; Illinois State Penitentiary of Joliet, Ill.; Cannon Mills Co. of Kannapolis, N.C.; Lone Star Cotton Mills of El Paso, Tex.; and Harmony Grove Mills of Commerce, Ga.

The cotton and paper industries did major battle for the packaging business in the late 1940's. Needless to say, the paper multiwalled bag came out the winner. The paper industry claimed that their bags, constructed of four walls of heavy Kraft paper, provided the best in price and sanitation. In 1948, the paper industry had taken over 53% of the shipping-sack market. During 1948, bag buyers could buy three multiwall one hundred pound paper bags for little more than the price of one cotton bag. Raw cotton prices ran from 10¢ a pound before World War II to about 36¢ a pound in 1948. Unbleached wood pulp increased from 3¼¢ a pound to about 6¢ a pound. Cotton bags cost 32¢ for a one hundred pound bag verses 10¢ for the same size paper bag.

Cotton, one of the four natural textile fibers, has been grown and produced in America since the 1600's when the first cotton plantations were established in Virginia. After Eli Whitney invented the cotton gin in 1793, cotton production rose in the United States. Cotton is often called the universal textile fiber and it is known for its natural comfort. The cycle of cotton begins with the cotton seeds being planted in the rich, dark soil during the early spring months. The picking or harvesting of the cotton begins in August and runs through the fall months. All cotton was picked by hand until 1936 when John and Mack Rust brought out their mechanical cotton picker. The individual that picked the cotton pulled a cotton pick sack to put the cotton in. The cotton pick sack, the largest cotton textile bag made, had a strap that went over the picker's shoulder.

Cotton Picking 1920

After the picker got his sack full of cotton, he would go "weigh up." Usually a scale and pee (the weight) were used for the weighing of the cotton. The sack of cotton was weighed, then the same was weighed empty and its weight was subtracted from the total weight. The weight of the cotton was written down in a cotton tally book. At the end of the day or week the farmer would pay his workers for the amount of cotton they had picked. During the 1950's, a worker was paid 3¢ for every pound of cotton he picked.

Weighing the cotton

Cotton Tally Books

After the cotton has been picked, the cotton is taken to a cotton gin by the trailer or wagon load. There the seed and foreign matter are removed from the cotton. The cotton is then compressed into bales weighing about 500 pounds. The cotton bale usually measures 54x27x27 inches.

This picture is of a press used to press cotton into bales. Picture courtesy of I.J. Hurdle Gin of Slayden, Mississippi.

This picture shows bales of cotton ready to be shipped to the textile mills. Picture courtesy of I.J. Hurdle Gin of Slayden, Mississippi.

From the cotton gin, the bales of cotton are shipped to the textile mills where it is processed into yarn. After World War I, textile mills began an exodus from New England, New York and Pennsylvania to the South. Before this time, most cotton was shipped to the Northeast.

Cotton yarns are woven into fabrics by the same basic principle as on the first handweaving frames. Modern looms work at great speeds. They interlace the lengthwise yarns, or warp, and the crosswise yarns, or filling. The woven fabric, called grey goods, is sent to a finishing plant where it is bleached, pre-shrunk, dyed, printed and given the type of finish desired.

Then the fabric is sent to the bag manufacturer where the cotton textile bags are made. Some of the textile bag manufacturers controlled their operations from cotton field to the finished bags. Bemis Brothers Bag Company and Fulton Bag and Cotton Mills of Atlanta, Ga. had their own textile mills where they produced the fabric they used in the manufacture of the textile bags. The manufacturer of the cotton textile bags was a big industry during the 1920's, 1930's, 1940's and 1950's. Competition was strong between leading bag manufacturers.

Names of some bag manufacturers will appear over and over on the textile bags that are collected. But some of the bags from the past will not have the name of any company on them. A brief history, pictures of early factories and pictures of bags manufactured by leading bag companies will be found on the following pages.

The building Chase - St. Louis
occupied circa 1870.

Chase Bag Company began in a rented loft on the Boston water-front with Henry S. Chase as the founder in 1847. In 1866, Chase opened a factory in St. Louis to serve the fast growing needs of the midwest. Chase opened a third plant in Kansas City in 1872.

Four bag companies merged with Chase Bag Company in 1925: The Northern Bag Company of Minneapolis; Milwaukee Bag Company; American Bag Company of Memphis, Tennessee; and The Cleveland-Akron Bag Company. This gave Chase Bag Company a nationwide network of bag plants. This same year, 1925, saw additions of the New Orleans and Toledo plants. In 1930, Chase purchased the Philadelphia Bag Company. Chase Bag Company began production of the multiwall paper bags in 1931 at its Chagrin Falls plant. The multiwall bag would be produced more and more by Chase during the years to follow. Chase Bag Company is one of the oldest bag manufacturers and today it is one of the major manufacturers in the packaging business.

First Bemis Factory, 1858

Judson Moss Bemis founded Bemis Brother Bag Company in 1858 in St. Louis, Missouri with four employees (a pressman, a machinest and two girls to operate the sewing machines). After one week of experience, the two girls could sew 400 half-barrel size bags a day. Bemis expanded with a second factory in Minneapolis. Other branches were added in Omaha, Chicago, Indianapolis, New Orleans, San Francisco, Memphis, Kansas City, Seattle, Houston and Winnipeg, Manitoba. By the end of the nineteenth century and the beginning of the twentieth century, the Bemis Brother Bag Company was the largest concern of its kind in the world. Bemis had a complete network of factories across the nation.

The most interesting project of the Bemis Company was the model industrial town of Bemis, Tennessee in Madison County. The company town was just a few miles from Jackson, Tennessee. The town was developed around the cotton mill which was built in 1900.

For many years the trademark of the company was a cat looking out of a bag. Many bags from the past bear the prestigious name of Bemis. Bemis Company, Inc. is one of the largest manufacturers in the packaging industry today.

Some ads used to promote the Kenprint and specialty textile bags.

Percy Kent Bag Company, Inc. was founded in 1885 in Brooklyn, New York by Percy Kent. This company furnished cotton textile bags to the east coast and near midwest at that time. Flour, sugar and feed bags made up the bulk of their business. Percy Kent Bag Company opened a company in Kansas City, Missouri that became one of the largest textile plants in the country. This plant produced primarily specialty cotton bags – pastel bags (Kentex), print bags (Kenprints), pillowcase bags, apron bags, terry cloth bags, bags with wash cloths and/or towels sewn into the bottom for premiums. It was during this time that "Semper Aliquid Novum" – (Always Something New) became the company's motto. In 1954, Percy Kent opened a new plant in Kansas City, Missouri. It was to produce both multiwall paper bags and textile bags.

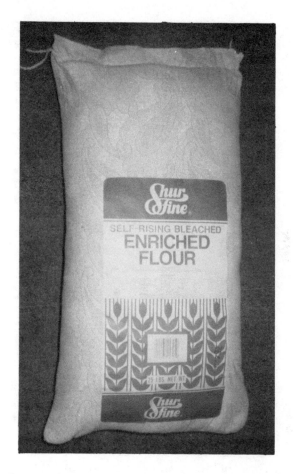

Percy Bag Company is still a major company in the packaging business and is one of the few bag manufacturers that still produces cotton textile flour bags. The picture shows a 25 pound bag of flour that can be bought at stores today. The bag was made by Percy Kent Bag Company.

Fulton Bag and Cotton Mills was established by Jacob Elsas in 1863 in Atlanta, Georgia. The company continued in business until 1957 at which time it was sold to W.J. Slifer. The company now operates under the name Fulton-Denver Company located in Denver, Colorado. Today, the Fulton-Denver Company is a major manufacturer of textile bags of burlap and various woven polyethylene configurations. The two beautifully printed bags shown here were produced by them.

Werthan Industries, Incorporated of Nashville, Tennessee bagan manufacturing bags about 1900. At that time it had branches in Houston, St. Louis and New Orleans. Werthan manufactured the colorful print bags as well as the white and solid colored bags. The company did all the printing on the bags. Werthan Industries now manufactures mostly paper and plastic bags for companies like Martha White and Ralston Purina. The two well printed bags shown here were manufactured by Werthan.

Central Bag Company was established in 1931 and has been operated by the Silverman family. The Central Bag Company, still in the packaging business today, is located in Kansas City, Missouri. The colorful meal bag was manufactured by them.

Langston Bags of Memphis, Tennessee has been manufacturing cotton textile bags since about 1946. Their name will be found on many of the bags that are collected. Langston Bags is still in the packaging business and manufactured the bag shown here.

Semmes Bag Company of Memphis, Tennessee has been manufacturing textile bags for several years. Their square logo will be seen on many of the bags that are collected. The Semmes Bag Company, now a part of McDowell Industries, manufactured the bag shown here.

Hutchinson Bag Corporation was established in Hutchinson, Kansas in the early 1920's. The corporation originally made salt pockets for the local salt companies of Hutchinson. They began supplying numerous little elevators across Kansas with cotton and burlap flour and feed bags. The corporation continued to grow and today holds a major place in the packaging industry. Hutchinson Bag Corporation still produces cotton bags for customers over most of the continental U.S. They made the bag pictured here.

Halsted Corporation of Jersey City, New Jersey was founded in 1876 by E.S. Halsted. This corporation produced cotton and burlap bags in its early years. Now some 113 years later, this corporation is still a major producer of packaging materials. The photos show a bag sent by Halsted Corporation on its 100th anniversary along with a printed invitation to its celebration. This is a very unique cotton textile bag since the invitation was enclosed.

Most of the bag companies discussed in this chapter began in the nineteenth century and remain giants in their field today. There were many bag manufacturers during the period that the cotton textile bags were popular. Many of the companies no longer exist or they have merged with other companies. The companies discussed in this chapter will become very familiar to the collector of the textile bags. Collecting bags from the different manufacturers can become a fascinating hobby.

# CHAPTER 3

## FLOUR MILLING AND FLOUR TEXTILE BAGS

Wheat was brought to the new world by Columbus, but attempts to grow it seemed to fail. The early English Colonists were the first wheat growers in North America and also the first flour millers. A grist mill was built at Jamestown about 1621. This was one of the first grist mills in the United States. Around 1870, almost all cities had flour mills and many cities had several. Practically every community had its own grist mill.

As our population moved westward, so did the bag manufacturers and milling companies. Baltimore was the center for flour milling in the early 1800's. By the late 1800's, the flour milling center had become St. Louis, Missouri.

Flour milling was long the most important industry in our nation. The flour milling business was the largest user of the textile bags for over fifty years. Flour is packaged in the multiwall paper bag today. Export flour is still shipped in the cotton bags. The exact date of when a flour textile bag was manufactured is sometimes hard to determine. Certain information can help to determine the date. If it were enriched flour, it was probably manufactured after 1941 when enriched flour became nationwide. The measurements help to establish a time of manufacture also. Even measurements of 2, 5, 10, 25, 50 and 100 pounds became standard in 1943. The measurements other than these six were usually used before that time. The time that the flour milling company was in business will also help date the bag. The same is true of when the bag manufacturer was in business.

The pictures, descriptions and pricing of the following flour textile bags are a sampling of the many flour bags that were produced during the years past and a sampling of the many milling companies that existed across our nation.

Two pounds of SELF ACTION Self Rising Flour came in this cotton textile bag. The flour was milled by the Cadick Milling Company of Grand View, Indiana. This milling company was established in 1900 and ceased to mill flour in 1948. The bag measures 9 by 6 inches. This type small well printed textile bag will sell for $16 to $18.

Nine and 8/10 pounds of GRAHAM Flour came in this white textile bag. The flour was milled by the Sperry Flour Company of San Francisco, California. The Sperry Flour Company was founded in 1852 and operated until 1929 when it was acquired by General Mills, Inc. The bag measures 14x10 inches. Since this bag has a very unusual measurement, it will sell for $24 to $26.

Ten pounds of SOUTHERN QUEEN Self-Rising Flour came in this print cotton textile bag. The bag measures 17x10½ inches. This bag was manufactured by the Fulton Bag Company of St. Louis. The flour was milled by the C. Becker Milling Company of Red Bud, Ill. The C. Becker Milling Company was established in 1894 and operated until 1952. This bag will sell for $30 to $32.

This 12 pound cotton textile bag held ASCENSION Self-Rising Flour milled by the Pinckneyville Milling Co. of Pinckneyville, Ill. Founded in 1871, the Pickneyville Milling Co. ceased to operate by 1950. The Bemis Brother Bag Company manufactured the 12 pound bag measuring 17½x11 inches. This is a well printed bag and will sell for $34 to $36.

This 10 pound print textile bag held WHITE RING All Purpose Flour. The flour was milled by the H.C. Cole Milling Co. of Chester, Illinois. The H.C. Cole Company was established in 1839. The bag measures 18x10 inches. This bag will sell for $14 to $16.

Ten pounds of AIRLIGHT Self-Rising Flour came in this print cotton textile bag. The flour was milled by the H.C. Cole Milling Co. of Chester, Ill. The H.C. Cole Co. was founded by Nathan Cole in 1839. The bag was manufactured by the Werthan Bag Co. of Nashville, Tennessee and measures 18x10½ inches and will sell for $14 to $16.

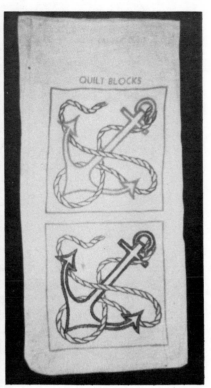

Front                                    Back

24 pounds of HEARD'S BEST Flour came in this white cotton textile
bag. The flour was produced by Raymond Heard Inc. of Ruston, Louisiana. The bag was manufactured by Percy Kent Bag Co. This is a
specialty bag with needlework back-prints. The back-prints could be
used for quilt blocks or pillow designs. The bag measures 24x12½
inches. This bag has the quilt blocks on the back plus the 24 pound
weight. It will sell for $46 to $48.

24 pounds of LADY CLAIR Self Rising Flour came in this well printed textile bag. Cumberland Valley Flour Co. of Nashville, Tenn. milled the flour. Werthan Bag Corp. of Nashville manufactured the bag. The bag measures 26x12½ inches. This 24 pound weight bag will sell for $30 to $32.

24 pounds of bleached INDIAN GIRL Pure Wheat Flour came in this white cotton textile bag. The flour was milled by Williamsville Roller Mill Co. of Williamsville, Mo. Bemis Brother Bag Company of St. Louis, Missouri manufactured the sack. This bag measures 25x12 inches and will sell for $25 to $27.

24½ pounds and 98 pounds of flour came in these two SLEEPY EYE Flour bags. The flour was milled by Sleepy Eye Milling Co. of Sleepy Eye, Minn. This company was established in 1883 and ceased to operate in 1921. According to Martin, the 24½ pound flour bag in beautiful colors of yellow, pink, green and purple sell in the price range of $300 to $400 if found. The white flour bags with black printing will sell for less.

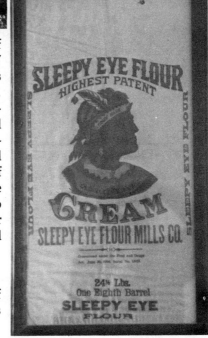

Pictures courtesy of Jim Martin of Monmouth, Illinois. Mr. Martin is president of Old Sleepy Eye.

25 pounds of AMERICAN BEAUTY Flour came in both these print cotton textile bags. The Russell-Miller Milling Company of Minneapolis milled the flour. Bemis Brother Bag Company manufactured the bags. Russell-Miller Milling Co. was founded in 1897 and continued in business until 1954 when it was acquired by the Peavey interests. The bags measure 24x13 inches. These spot labeled bags will sell for $20 to $22.

25 pounds of WHITE RING ALL PURPOSE FLOUR came in the print cotton textile bag. The H.C. Cole Milling Co. of Chester, Ill. milled the flour. This company was founded in 1839. The Werthan Bag Corporation of Nashville, Tenn. manufactured the bag. This spot labeled bag had free coupons packed inside the flour bag. Once enough coupons had been saved, a coffee pot, clock, camera or radio could be obtained free. The bag measures 27½x13 inches. The bag is in excellent condition and will sell for $20 to $22.

25 pounds of BANNOCK CHIEF Flour came in this white striped cotton textile bag. The flour was milled by the Peavey Flour Company of Minneapolis. The bag was manufactured by the Hutchinson Bag Corp. The bag measures 26½x12½ inches and will sell for $18 to $20.

This 25 pound WHITE RING All Purpose Flour bag became a ready to use pillowcase by just ripping out one seam. This pillowcase bag was manufactured by the Percy Kent Bag Company. The flour was milled by the H.C. Cole Milling Company of Chester, Illinois. H.C. Cole Milling Co. was established in 1839. This bag measures 28x20 inches. Since this is a specialty bag that is just like it came from the factory, it will sell for $60 to $62.

25 pounds of OMEGA Pure Soft Wheat Flour came in this white cotton textile bag. The bag was a shantung bag already hemmed. All the housewife had to do was rip the bag apart and she had a ready to use tea towel. The bag was manufactured by the Percy Kent Bag Co. H.C. Cole Milling Co. milled the flour. The bag measures 26x13 inches and will sell for $30 to $32.

25 pounds of WHITE RING Self Rising Flour came in this textile bag. This bag has a spot label on it. H.C. Cole Milling Company of Chester, Illinois milled the flour. The Semmes Bag Company of Memphis, Tenn. manufactured the bag. The bag measures 26x12½ inches and will sell for $14 to $16.

25 pounds of OMEGA Soft Wheat Flour came in this white textile bag. The H.C. Cole Milling Company of Chester, Ill. milled the flour. This company was established in 1839. Bemis Brother Bag Company manufactured the bag. The printed instructions at the top of the bag tell how to wash out the printing so the bag can be reused. The bag measures 26x12 inches and will sell for $20 to $22.

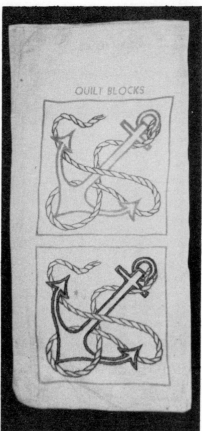

| Front | Back |

25 pounds of SHAWNEE'S BEST Flour came in this textile bag. The flour was produced by the Shawnee Milling Co. of Shawnee, Okla. The company was established in 1906 and burned in 1934. The bag was manufactured by Chase Bag Co. of Dallas, Texas. The bag has two quilt blocks on the back. The bag measures 26x12½ inches. This bag, with the quilt blocks on the back, will sell for $50 to $52.

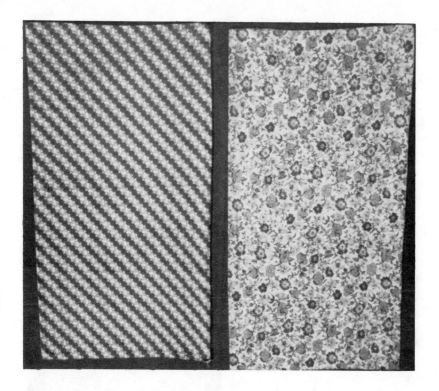

These bags are 25 pound cotton print textile bags with the labels missing. Since the labels are missing, they will not sell for as much as the ones with labels. Both these bags measure 24x13 inches. The bags would sell for $10 to $12.

This 48 pounds of SWANS DOWN FLOUR was milled by the Igleheart Brothers, Inc. of Evansville, IN. The Igleheart Brothers was founded in 1856 and acquired by General Foods Corp. in 1926. Fulton Bag and Cotton Mills manufactured the bag. This bag measures 29x15¼ inches. This is a bag with an odd measurement and beautiful printing. It will sell for $60 to $62.

48 pounds of BLUE RIBBON Plain Flour came in this white cotton textile bag. The flour was milled by the Washington Flour Mill of Washington, MO. Chase Bag Company manufactured the bag measuring 31x15½ inches. It will sell for $22 to $24.

49 pounds of TOWN CRIER Flour came in this white textile bag. The flour was milled by the Midland Flour Milling Company of Kansas City, MO. This company was founded in 1919 and was sold in 1943. The bag measures 29x15 inches and will sell for $28 to $30.

This 50 pounds of FAIRYLAN Self Rising Flour was milled by the Russell Company of Jackson, MS. Semmes Bag Company of 'Memphis, TN manufactured the white, spot labeled bag measuring 29x16½ inches. This bag is in excellent condition and will sell for $16 to $18.

50 pounds of All Purpose MILKWHITE FLOUR came in this white cotton textile bag with the band label. The flour was milled by Intermountain Farmers Association of Salt Lake City, Ut. The bag measures 29x17 inches and will sell for $16 to $18.

50 pounds of ROSE Self Rising Flour came in this white cotton textile bag. The flour was milled by All Star Mills, Inc. of Albemarle, NC. The bag, manufactured by Werthan Bag Corp. of Nashville, TN, measures 30x16½ inches. This well printed bag is in excellent condition and will sell for $18 to $20.

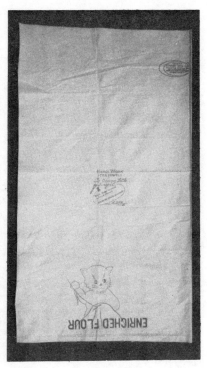

Front                                          Back

50 pounds of RUSSELL'S BEST Enriched Flour came in this white
cambric cloth bag. A "Handi Work Tea Towel Design" to be embroidered was on the back. The Russell Milling Co. of Russell, Kansas milled the flour. This company was established in 1906 and was
sold in 1943. Chase Bag Co. of Kansas City manufactured the bag.
The bag measures 30x17 inches. This bag, with the design on the back,
will sell for $30 to $32.

Front                                    Back

98 pounds of BLAIR'S CERTIFIED Flour came in this white cotton
textile bag. The flour was milled by The Blair Milling Company of
Atchison, Kansas. This company was established in 1866. There was
a Certified Pig Doll on the back of the bag. This bag measures 34x16
inches and will sell for $28 to $30 since the doll is printed on the back.

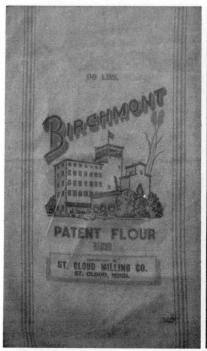

Pictures courtesy of Russell W. Carpenter of Coon Rapids, Iowa.

98 pounds of BIRCHMONT Flour came in this bag. The flour was milled by the St. Cloud Milling Co. of St. Cloud, Minn. The bag is a FULTON Seamless A Junior Size bag. It was manufactured by the Fulton Bag Company. This bag is rare in two ways. It is a 98 pound bag and it is a junior size seamless A bag. The bag measures 36x20 inches. This bag will sell for $75 to $80.

98 pounds of KING HUBBARD Flour was packaged in this textile bag. The Hubbard Milling Company of Mankato, MN milled the flour. The Hubbard Company was established in 1879 by R.D. Hubbard. The bag was manufactured by the Bemis Brother Bag Co. and measures 33x19 inches. This well printed bag will sell for $30 to $32.

Picture courtesy of Sherrye and Robert Livingston of Boston, Mass.

100 pounds of WASHBURN CROSBY GOLD MEDAL IRON DUKE Bleached Flour came in this white textile bag. The flour was milled by General Mills, Inc. of Minneapolis, MN. Percy Kent Bag Co., Inc. manufactured the bag. The bag measures 33x18 inches and will sell for $30 to $32.

100 pounds of GOLD DOLLARS Flour came in this white textile bag. The Aetna Mills milled the flour. The bag measures 33x18 inches and will sell for $12 to $14.

100 pounds of AUNT JEMIMA Flour came in this white textile bag. The Quaker Oats Company of Chicago milled the flour. Aunt Jemima Mills was founded in 1914. It merged with Quaker Oats Company in 1925. The bag measures 37x23 inches and will sell for $60 to $62.

100 pounds of export flour was shipped in this white textile bag. The VALIANT Winter Wheat Flour was milled by The Pillsbury Company of Minneapolis, MN. The United Bags, Inc. of St. Louis, MO manufactured the bag. The bag measures 33½x20 inches and will sell for $18 to $20.

This 100 pound white textile bag is a modern day (1984) export bag for flour. The KANSAS DIAMOND Flour was milled by the Dixie Portland Flour Mills, Inc. of Memphis, TN. The well printed export bag measures 35x20½ inches and will sell for $16 to $18.

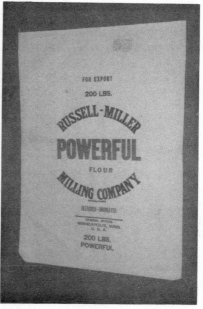

200 pounds of export flour was shipped in these two bags. The flour
was milled by the Russell-Miller Milling Company of Minneapolis,
Minn. This company was established in 1897 and was sold to the
Peavy interests in 1954. The bags were manufactured by Bemis Brother
Bag Company. The bags each measure 40x29 inches. These large
export bags will sell for $24 to $26.

Flour was packaged in textile bags ranging in size from the small 2 pound bag to the large 200 pound export bags. The flour that came in these bags was all-purpose or self-rising, made from soft wheat or hard wheat and was either enriched or not enriched.

Flour was a product that every home needed during the years that the textile bags were so popular. Most housewives made their bread, cakes and pies and this called for the buying of flour, usually in textile bags. The flour bags were discarded by few ladies of the house. This was a time when thrift was a very outstanding trait in Americans. Many children reared during these years remember wearing underwear with Pillsbury's Best written on them. The flour bags were used for making everything from underwear for family members to curtains for the kitchen windows.

Collecting flour sacks is an easy area in which to collect because so many flour sacks were made and there are still many out there to be found.

## TEXTILE FLOUR BAGS NOT PICTURED

10 pound flour cotton textile bag that held DRIFTED SNOW Roller Process Flour. The Sperry Flour Company milled the flour. This bag measures 17½x9 inches .......................... $16 to $18

10 pound flour cotton textile bag that held SNOW LILY Flour. The bag measures 17x9½ inches and has green strips at the top and bottom ................................................. $10 to $12

24 pound flour cotton textile bag that held BEST Flour. The Curtis Mills of Curtis and Crete, Nebraska milled the flour. The bag maeasures 25x12 inches .......................... $18 to $20

49 pound flour cotton textile bag that held CERETANA Flour. The Montana Flour Mills Co. of Bozeman-Great Falls-Harlowton-Lewistown, Montana milled the flour. This bag measures 30x15 inches ................................................. $18 to $20

50 pound flour cotton textile bag that held OUR FAMILY Flour. The Nash-Finch Co. of Minneapolis, Minn. milled the flour. The bag has red, yellow, blue and green strips and measures 29x15½ inches ................................................. $12 to $14

50 pound print cotton textile bag that held JACK SPRAT Flour. Jack Sprat Foods Inc. manufactured the flour. This bag has a band label and measures 29x16 inches ........................ $18 to $20

# CHAPTER 4

## THE SUGAR INDUSTRY AND SUGAR TEXTILE BAG

Sugar, Sugar, Sugar! The wonderful sweet taste of sugar appeals to almost everyone. The housewife has been carrying sugar home for centuries in every measurement from a cupful to a 100 pound bag. Fierce pirates of long ago considered sugar almost as valuable as gold. Christopher Columbus brought sugar cane to Santo Domingo on his second voyage in 1494. From Santo Domingo, it spread to other areas like Cuba and South America. The production of raw sugar in tropical America was a great industry by 1600. In 1751, the Jesuit Fathers of Santo Domingo brought the cultivation of sugar cane to Louisiana. The sugar industry flourished in Louisiana and that state still remains as the leading sugar cane area in the Continental United States. Hawaii is the top sugar state in the nation.

The sugar industry used the cotton textile bags to package its sugar until they were outdated by the multiwalled paper bag. About 20% of the cotton textile bags manufactured were used by the sugar industry. These bags were usually white cotton and in measurements of 5, 10, 25, 50 and 100 pound weights. Many of the sugar bags were labeled "Towel Bags". These sugar bags had a red and blue stripe on each side of the bag and were made for reuse by the thrifty housewife. After the sugar bag was empty, the lady of the house ripped the seam apart, washed the lettering from the bag and then hemmed the raw edges. Presto, she had a cotton dish towel, tea towel or hand towel.

The U.S. imports about half of the sugar it uses from foreign countries. Before 1960, the largest part of this sugar was imported from Cuba. After 1960, the U.S. would not allow Cuban sugar into this country because of policies of the Cuban government. Many of the sugar bags collected today will have "A Product of Cuba" written on the bag. These bags entered the U.S. before 1960.

Generations ago, the housewife carried home more sugar than does the housewife of today. Today, many of our foods already have sugar in them like cereal, soda, cake mixes, etc. The housewife of years past used sugar for preserving and canning foods for her family. She made all her desserts from scratch and she needed sugar for these recipes.

Many of the names of sugar companies found on the bags collected today no longer exist. A few major sugar companies were founded in the 1800's and continue in business today. Pictures of the sugar bags on the following pages are a sample of the different bag measurements and different sugar companies that manufactured the sugar.

51

2 pounds of C and H Pure Cane Berry Granulated Sugar came in this small textile bag. The sugar was manufactured by the California and Hawaiian Sugar Refining Corp. of San Francisco. This bag measures 5x10 inches and has a copyright date of 1939 on the back. This bag will sell for $14 to $16.

5 pounds of WHITE SATIN Sugar came in this white cotton textile bag. The sugar was produced by The Amalgamated Sugar Company of Ogden, UT. The bag measures 13x7 inches. This small well printed bag would sell for $10 to $12.

25 pounds and 5 pounds of DOMINO Pure Cane Sugar came in these two cotton textile bags. The Domino brand of sugar can still be purchased today in multiwalled paper bags. The sugar was manufactured by the American Sugar Refining Company of New York, NY. The 25 pound bag measures 19x12½ inches and will sell for $20 to $22. The 5 pound bag measures 12x7½ inches and will sell for $10 to $12.

10 pounds of REVERE Granulated Cane Sugar came in this white textile bag. The sugar was manufactured by the Revere Sugar Refinery of Boston, MA. This bag is printed on the back with directions for opening the bag. This bag measures 16x9 inches. This sugar bag with a picture of Revere on it will sell for $30 to $32.

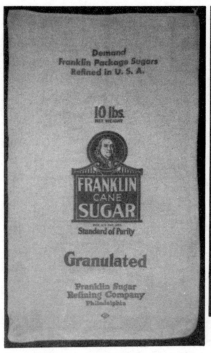

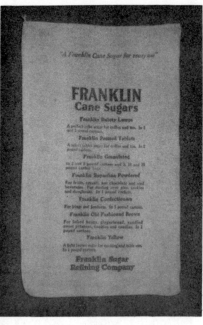

Back

Front

10 pounds of FRANKLIN Cane Sugar came in this textile bag. The sugar was produced by the Franklin Sugar Refining Company of Philadelphia. The back of the sack is well printed with interesting information. The bag measures 15½x9½ inches. Since the bag has a picture of Franklin himself on the bag, the bag will sell for $24 to $26.

Front                                          Back

10 pounds of McCahan's SUNNY Cane Sugar came in this white textile bag. The W.J. McCahan Sugar Refining and Molasses Co. of Philadelphia, PA produced the sugar. The back of this bag is well printed also. The bag measures 16x9 inches. This bag is in excellent condition and will sell for $16 to $18.

Front                                      Back

10 pounds of JACK FROST Cane Sugar came in this textile bag. The sugar was produced by The National Sugar Refining Co. of New Jersey. The back of this bag is well printed. The bag measures 16x9 inches. This bag will sell for $16 to $18.

10 pounds of QUAKER Pure Cane Sugar came in this textile bag. The sugar was produced by the Pennsylvania Sugar Co. of Philadelphia, PA. The copyright date on the 16x9 inch bag is 1930. This bag would sell for $20 to $22.

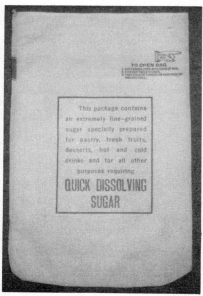

| Front | Back |

10 pounds of U and I Extra Fine Granulated Sugar came in this textile bag. The sugar was produced by the Utah-Idaho Sugar Company of Salt Lake City, Utah. The bag measures 15x10½ inches. This bag will sell for $12 to $14.

10 pounds of CRYSTAL SUGAR came in this cotton textile bag. The American Crystal Sugar Co. of Mason City, IA refined this sugar. The bag measures 15x9½ inches and will sell for $12 to $14.

10 pounds of SEA ISLAND Sugar came in this white textile bag. The sugar was refined by the Western Sugar Refinery of San Francisco, California. The Western Sugar Co. was established in 1863. The bag pictured above was stamped with the pattern for making a doll. The customer had only to cut the doll out, sew it up and stuff. This doll was a "TRILI" Swiss Girl Doll. This bag has a copyright date of 1936 and measures 16x10½ inches. There was a series of dolls printed on Sea Island Sugar bags at this time. Pictures of 3 other doll sugar sacks follow. Since this bag has a printed doll on it and it was produced in the 1930's, the bag will sell for $44 to $46. The doll will sell for $20 to $22.

Front

Back

10 pounds of SEA ISLAND SUGAR came in this white textile bag. The sugar was refined by the Western Sugar Refinery of San Francisco, California. The company was established in 1863. This bag has a pattern for the "TONIO" Italian Doll printed on it. This 1936 bag measures 16x10½ inches. This bag is a special printed one and will sell for $44 to $46.

10 pounds of GODCHAUX Pure Cane Sugar came in this white textile bag. Notice that this bag has the raw seam outside so the sugar will not get thread ravelings in it. This bag has a copyright date of 1939 and measures 17x9 inches. The sugar was refined by the Godchaux Sugars, Inc. of New Orleans, LA. The bag measures 17x9 inches. Since this bag has a raw outside seam, it would sell for $30 to $32.

59

| Front | Back |
|:---:|:---:|

10 pounds of SEA ISLAND SUGAR came in this white textile bag. The sugar was refined by the Western Sugar Refinery of San Francisco, California. The company was established in 1863. This bag has a pattern for the "JONG-YI" Korean Doll printed on it and a copyright date of 1936. The bag measures 16x10½ inches. This will printed bag with the doll pattern on it would sell for $44 to $46.

10 pounds of Pure GREAT WESTERN Granulated Sugar came in this white cotton bag. The sugar was manufactured by the Great Western Sugar Co. of Denver, CO. The bag measures 14x9½ inches and will sell for $12 to $14.

|  Front  |  Back  |
| --- | --- |

10 pounds of SEA ISLAND SUGAR came in this white textile bag. The sugar was refined by the Western Sugar Refinery of San Francisco, California. This company was established in 1863. This sugar bag has a pattern for the "ILEANA" Rumanian Doll printed on it and a copyright date of 1936. The bag measures 16x10½ inches. This bag has been specially printed with the doll pattern and would sell for $44 to $46.

This textile bag held 10 pounds of WHITE GOLD Pure Cane Sugar at one time. The South Coast Corp. of New Orleans refined the sugar. The bag, well printed on both sides, measures 15½x10 inches. This bag will sell for $12 to $14.

10 pounds of HOLLY Pure Granulated Sugar came in this white textile bag. The sugar was refined by the Holly Sugar Corporation of Colorado Springs, CO. The bag measures 15x9 inches and will sell for $10 to $12.

100 pounds of C and H Sugar came in this white textile bag. The California and Hawaiian Sugar Refining Corporation of San Francisco, CA refined the sugar. This bag measures 35x19 inches. The bag will sell for $22 to $24.

100 pounds and 10 pounds of GODCHAUX'S Sugar came in these two white textile bags. The sugar was refined by Godchaux Sugars, Inc. of Reserve, LA. The company was founded in 1862 by Leon Godchaux from Herbeville, France when he purchased "LaReserve" Plantation at Reserve, LA. The apron is an advertising apron given by the company. The 100 pound bag measures 36x19 inches. The 10 pound bag measures 16x10 inches. The 100 pound bag will sell for $30 to $32. The 10 pound bag will sell for $20 to $22. The apron will sell for $24 to $26.

100 pounds of COLONIAL Sugar came in these two white textile bags. The Colonial Sugars Co. of New Orleans, LA refined this standard fine granulated sugar. The Colonial Sugars Co. was founded around 1900 and acquired by Savannah Foods and Industries of Savannah, GA in 1986. These bags measure 34x18 inches. The first bag pictured is a towel bag with the red and blue stripes and it will sell for $34 to $36. The second bag pictured will sell for $40 to $42 because of the well printed picture.

100 pounds of C and H Pure Cane Sugar came in this white textile bag. The sugar was manufactured by the California and Hawaiian Sugar Refining Corp. Ltd. of San Francisco, CA. This bag measures 36x18 inches and will sell for $18 to $20.

100 pounds of SPRECKELS Sugar came in this Honey-Dew Brand textile bag. The sugar was refined by the Spreckels Sugar Co. of San Francisco, CA. The bag measures 34x18½ inches and will sell for $14 to $16.

100 pounds of STERLING Quality Pure Cane Sugar came in this white textile bag. Sterling Sugars Inc. of Franklin, LA manufactured the sugar. Fulton Bags of New Orleans manufactured the 34x17 inch bag. This bag will sell for $20 to $22.

100 pounds of GREAT WESTERN Pure Sugar came in this cotton textile bag. The sugar was refined by the Great Western Sugar Co. of Denver, CO. This bag measures 34x20 inches. This bag is in excellent condition and will sell for $20 to $22.

100 pounds of DIXIE CRYSTALS Pure Cane Sugar came in this cotton towel bag. The sugar was refined by Savannah Sugar Refinery. The bag measures 33x18 inches. This towel bag will sell for $34 to $36.

100 pounds of HERSHEY'S Pure Cane Sugar came in this textile bag. The sugar was made in Central Hersey, Cuba for the Hershey Corporation of Hershey, PA, U.S.A. The bag measures 34x18 inches. This bag, since the sugar was manufactured in Cuba, will sell for $42 to $44.

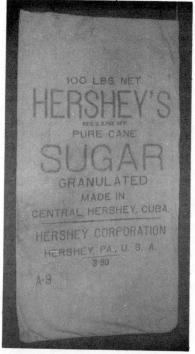

67

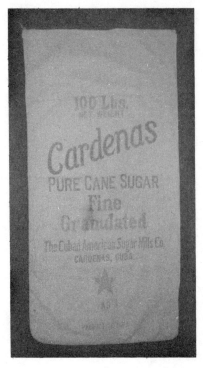

100 pounds of CARDENAS Pure Cane Sugar came in this cotton textile bag. The sugar was refined by the Cuban American Sugar Mills Co. of Cardenas, Cuba. The sugar was a product of Cuba and was imported before 1960. The bag measures 34x18 inches. Since this bag is from Cuba, it would sell for $40 to $42.

100 pounds of PEARL WHITE Sugar came in this white textile bag. The sugar was manufactured by the Matanzas Sugar Estates, Inc. of Cuba. The bag measures 34x18 inches. This bag, since the sugar came from Cuba, will sell for $44 to $46.

100 pounds of EVERSWEET Pure Cane Sugar came in this white textile bag. The sugar was manufactured by Compania Azucarera Del Camuy, Inc. of Camuy, Puerto Rico. The bag measures 33x19 inches. The bag, since it is from Puerto Rico, will sell for $40 to $42.

## TEXTILE SUGAR BAGS NOT PICTURED

25 pound sugar cotton textile bag that held JACK FROST Granulated Sugar. The National Sugar Refining Co. of New Jersey refined the sugar. This is a towel bag that measures 19x13 inches  $12 to $14

25 pound white sugar textile bag that held SEA ISLAND Sugar. The Western Refinery of San Francisco, Calif. refined the sugar. The bag, with clouds, trees and waves pictured on the front, measures 20x13 inches ........................................ $10 to $12

100 pound white textile bag that held MOUNTAIN Granulated Sugar. The bag measures 34½x18 inches .................. $18 to $20

100 pound white sugar textile bag that held Pure Cane Granulated Sugar. The sugar was refined by the Central San Cristobal, S.A. San Cristobal, Cuba. This Cuban sugar bag measures 34x18 inches .............................................. $40 to $42

100 pound white sugar textile bag that held Pure Granulated Sugar. The sugar was manufactured by Central Santa Isabel, Fomento, Las Villas, Cuba. The bag has palm trees pictured on the front and measures 34x18 inches ........................... $40 to $42

The sugar companies have not used the cotton textile bags in 15 to 20 years to package their sugar. They use the multiwalled paper bags like the DOMINO Sugar bag in the picture. Several weight measurements of sugar can be purchased from the grocery store today including 2, 5 and 10 pound bags. It is hard to find anything larger than 10 pounds of sugar on the grocery shelf. I have been unable to find sugar sold in the cotton textile bags anywhere.

The picture on the right shows the War Rations stamp books that were issued during World War II by the U.S. Government. The books had sugar, coffee, gas and other stamps in them. These stamps were used to buy these products during the rationing years of World War II.

Sugar was refined in many states across our nation even though the sugar cane is grown in only a few states. The cotton textile sugar bags are hard to find today because they were used many years ago, the housewife reused so many of them and there were fewer sugar bags manufactured than there were of flour.

# CHAPTER 5

## THE FEED INDUSTRY AND THE COTTON TEXTILE FEED BAGS

Fashion became an important factor at the feed stores across America. When the farmer or man of the house went to the feed store, he found himself taking swatches of cloth to be matched. The housewives were using the gay and attractive prints of the feed bags to dress their families and homes.

The feed bags were usually in the 50 and 100 pound bag sizes. The bags were filled with feed for animals living on farms. Feed companies used about 12% of the bags manufactured during this period. Feed was produced in every state in the U.S. and housewives all across America reused these beautifully printed feed bags. Feed bags in prints, stripes, squares, florals and checks were chosen by the housewife of this time.

100 pounds of B-B Poultry Rations came in this beautiful print textile bag. The Maritime Mlg. Co. of Buffalo, NY manufactured the feed. The bag measures 38x23 inches. This print, band labeled bag will sell for $50 to $52.

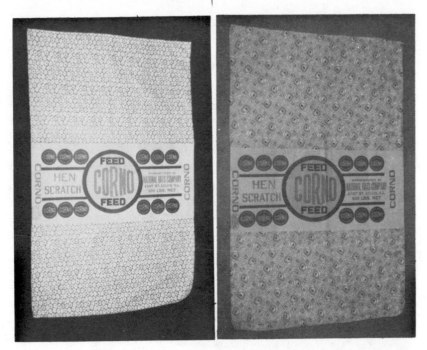

100 pounds of CORNO Hen Scratch Feed came in these two beautiful print textile bags. The National Oats Company of East St. Louis, IL manufactured the feed. Chase Bag Company manufactured the bags. They are Chase Pretty Print Banded Label Bags. The bags measure 34x22 inches. Each of these bags will sell for $50 to $52.

After the feed bags were emptied, the seam was ripped out, the bag was washed, starched and ironed, and then it was ready to be cut into dresses, shirts, aprons, housecoats and curtains. When the housewife didn't have enough feed bags of one print, she would trade feed bags with other housewives in her community. She could purchase just the empty bag from some feed stores. These cost from 5¢ to 15¢ each. The 100 pound feed bags were used to make adult wearing apparel. It usually took three 100 pound feed bags to make a lady's dress.

An estimated 34 million tons of manufactured feeds for livestock and poultry were produced in the United States in 1953. Some of this feed was delivered to the farms in bulk but most of the feeds were packed in cotton textile bags. Bags for a ton of feed cost the feed mill from $2 to $10. This was included in the price at which the feed was sold.

The feed bags pictured on the following pages are a sample of the different kinds of feed manufactured, the different companies that manufactured the feed and a price guide for the collector of the feed bags.

100 pounds of DOUBLE DIAMOND Feed came in this print textile bag. The feed was milled by the Daily Mills, Inc. of Olean, NY. This beautiful print bag measures 38x23 inches and will sell for $50 to $52.

100 pounds of PURINA FLOCK CHOW was packaged in this gay print textile bag. The bag was manufactured by Bemis Brother Bag Company. It is a Bemis Band-Label Bag. The bag measures 38x24 inches and will sell for $50 to $52.

100 pounds of feed came in this print cotton textile bag. The bag no longer has a label on it, but it is still very collectible because of the bright, gay print. The bag measures 37x22 inches and will sell for $18 to $20.

50 pounds of SUNRISE Laying Mash came in this white cotton textile bag. The bag was manufactured by the Bemis Brother Bag Co. The laying mash was manufactured by Royal-Stafolife Mills of Memphis, TN. The bag measuring 29x16 inches will sell for $20 to $22.

Picture courtesy of
Montra W. Fletcher

50 pounds of LAY-MO HEN
SCRATCH FEED came in this
white textile bag. The feed was
manufactured by the Superior
Feed Co. of Memphis, TN and
Meridian, MS. Bemis Brother Bag
Co. manufactured the bag. The
bag measures 29x14 inches and
will sell for $20 to $22.

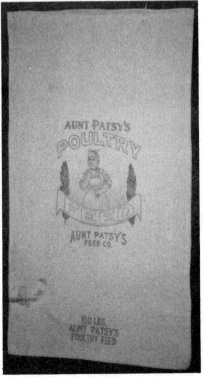

100 pounds of AUNT PATSY'S
POULTRY FEED came in this
white textile bag. The feed was
manufactured by Aunt Patsy's
Feed Co. The bag measures 39x22
inches. This bag is well printed
and will sell for $32 to $34.

76

100 pounds of Poultry Feed came in this textile bag. The feed was manufactured by The Quaker Oats Company of Chicago. The bag measures 38x18 inches. This bag, with the unusual picture of the chicken and clock, will sell for $40 to $42.

100 pounds of MERIT Poultry Feed came in this cotton textile bag. The feed was manufactured by Clark-Burkle and Co. of Memphis, TN. The bag measures 33x17½ inches. This bag, with the outstanding picture of the chickens, will sell for $40 to $42.

100 pounds of FUL-O-PEP Laying Mash came in this cotton textile bag. The feed was manufactured by The Quaker Oats Co. of Chicago. The bag measures 37x20 inches. This bag will sell for $34 to $36.

100 pounds of ARCHER BRAND Poultry Feeds came in this textile bag. Archer-Daniels-Midland Co. of Minneapolis, MN manufactured the feed. Percy Kent Bag Co. manufactured the bag. An issue date of June 2, 1942 is printed on the bag measuring 39x23 inches. This bag will sell for $24 to $26.

100 pounds of MASTER MIX Layer Concentrate came in this textile bag. The feed was manufactured by McMillen Feed Mills a division of Central Soya Company, Inc. Mills of Memphis, Tenn., Decatur, Ind., Gibson City, Ill., Harrisburg, Pa., and Marion, Ohio. The bag measures 38x20 inches and will sell for $18 to $20.

100 pounds of ALWAYS A-HEAD Scratch Feed came in this white cotton textile bag. The feed was manufactured by Black & White Milling Company of East St. Louis, IL. The bag was manufactured by Bemis - St. Louis. The bag measures 38x19½ inches. This red, white and blue printed bag will sell for $22 to $24.

100 pounds of ELMORE Growing Mash came in this white cotton textile bag. The mash was manufactured by the Elmore Milling Company, Inc. of Oneonta, NY. Percy Kent Bag Company manufactured this well printed bag which measures 36x22 inches. This bag will sell for $24 to $26.

Picture courtesy of
Sherry and Robert Livingston

100 pounds of SECURITY EGG MASH came in this textile bag. The feed was manufactured by Security Mills of Knoxville, TN. This well printed bag measures 38x20 inches and will sell for $24 to $26.

100 pounds of PURINA Flock Chow and Turkey Growena came in these two white cotton textile bags. The Purina Company manufactured the feed. Each bag measures 38x22 and will sell for $18 to $20.

100 pounds of SUNFED Gray Shorts came in this white cotton textile bag. The Larabee Flour Mills Company of Kansas City, MO manufactured the feed. The bag was manufactured by the Percy Kent Bag Co. The bag measures 38x20 inches and will sell for $18 to $20.

100 pounds of WHITE FROST Shorts came in this white cotton textile bag. This bag was double stitched to prevent sifting. The Model Milling Co. manufactured the feed. The bag measures 35x19 inches. This bag will sell for $16 to $18.

100 pounds of EASTER LILY Wheat Gray Shorts came in this white cotton textile bag. The shorts was milled by Trenton Milling Company of Trenton, IL. They also milled flour. The bag was manufactured by the B&B Company. The bag measures 38x21 inches. This beautifully printed bag will sell for $26 to $28.

100 pounds of Scott's Auburn LEADER Soft Winter Wheat Shorts came in this cotton textile bag. The feed was manufactured by The Auburn Mills, Inc. of Auburn, KY. The bag was manufactured by the Werthan Bag Corp. of Nashville. The bag measures 38x22 inches. This bag will sell for $14 to $16.

100 pounds of OMOR Wheat Shorts came in this cotton textile bag. The feed was milled by Omaha Flour Mills Co. of Denver, CO. Fulton Bags of Denver manufactured the bag. This bag measures 38x23 inches. This bag is in excellent condition and will sell for $26 to $28.

100 pounds of WAYNE Hog Supplement came in each of these white cotton textile bags. The Allied Mills, Inc. of Chicago, IL manufactured the feed. Bosworth Bags of Memphis, TN manufactured the bags. Each bag measures 38x20 inches and will sell for $24 to $26.

100 pounds of ARCHER BRAND Hog Balancer came in this white cotton textile bag. The feed was manufactured by the Archer-Daniels-Midland Company of Minneapolis, MN. An issue date of June 2, 1942 is printed on the bag manufactured by Bemis, St. L. The bag measures 39x21 inches and will sell for $24 to $26.

100 pounds of ECLIPSE 40% Hog Supplement came in this textile bag. The Eclipse Feed Mills, Inc. of Highland, IL manufactured the feed. The bag was manufactured by the Werthan Bag Corporation of Nashville and measures 39x20 inches. This bag will sell for $20 to $22.

100 pounds of CRITIC Quality Feeds of 40% Mineralized Hog Concentrate came in this cotton textile bag. Schultz, Baujan & Co. of Beardston, IL manufactured the feed. Schultz, Baujan & Co. opened their feed mill in 1929 and consolidated with Colorado Milling and Elevator Co. in 1953. Bemis Brother Bag Co. of St. Louis manufactured the bag. The cotton boll at the top of the bag has a printed address for ordering a free booklet that tells 100 ways to use the bag for household uses. The address given was: Textile Bags, 100 No. Lasalle St., Chicago, IL. The bag measures 37x21 inches and will sell for $26 to $28.

85

100 pounds of CANNON VALLEY Pure Hard Wheat Bran came in this bag. Cannon Valley Milling Co. of Minneapolis, MN with mills at Cannon Falls, MN manufactured the feed. Chase Bag Company manufactured the bag. The bag measures 38x23½ inches. This well printed bag with the cannon on it will sell for $30 to $32.

100 pounds of BLACKHAWK Wheat Bran came in this cotton textile bag. The International Milling Company of Minneapolis, MN and Buffalo, NY manufactured the feed. The bag measures 38x23 inches. This bag, with the great blackhawk on it, will sell for $44 to $46.

100 pounds of MOTHER'S BEST Quality Feeds of Pure Wheat Bran came in this cotton textile bag. This feed was a product of Mother's Best Flour Mills. The feed was distributed by Nebraska Consolidated Mills. Co. of Omaha, Fremont, Grand Island and Hastings, NE. The bag was manufactured by the Bemis Brother Bag Co. and measures 38x22½ inches. This well printed bag will sell for $50 to $52.

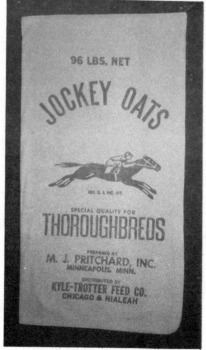

96 pounds of JOCKEY OATS, Special Quality For Thoroughbreds, came in this textile bag. The oats were prepared by M.J. Pritchard, Inc. of Minneapolis, MN and distributed by Kyle-Trotter Feed Co. of Chicago. The bag measures 38x21 inches. This bag has an odd measurement and is well printed. It will sell for $30 to $32.

100 pounds of RED ROSE Feeds came in these two cotton textile bags. 100 pounds of Turkey Grower came in one. Pig and Sow Meal came in the other. The feed was manufactured by John W. Eshelman and Sons of Lancaster and York, PA - Circleville, OH - Tampa, FL and Sanford, NC. John Eshelman and Sons was established in 1842. The bags each measure 38x22 inches and will sell for $24 to $26.

100 pounds of DIXIE Dairy Feed and Hog Feed came in these two white cotton textile bags. The Dixie Mills Co. of East St. Louis manufactured the feed. Bemis Bag Co. manufactured the bags. Each bag measures 38x23 inches and will sell for $18 to $20.

100 pounds of BULL BRAND Dairy Rations was packaged in this textile bag. Maritime Mlg. Co. Inc. of Buffalo, NY milled the feed. The bag measures 38x25 inches. This well printed bag will sell for $40 to $42.

100 pounds of S-X Feeds came in this textile bag. The feed was manufactured by the Essex County Co-Operative Farming Association, incorporated in 1917, of Topsfield, MA. This well printed bag measures 38x23 inches and will sell for $24 to $26.

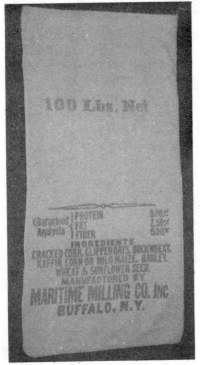

100 pounds of MARITIME Feed came in this white textile bag. The Maritime Milling Co. Inc. of Buffalo, NY manufactured the feed. The bag measures 37x18 inches. This bag will sell for $12 to $14.

100 pounds of T-SQUARE Yellow Corn Chops came in this textile bag. Thibault Milling Company of Little Rock, AR milled the feed. The Semmes Bag Company of Memphis, TN made the bag which measures 38x21 inches. This bag will sell for $16 to $18.

167 pounds of SWIFT'S Pure Champion Wheat and Corn Grower came in this seamless textile bag. The feed was manufactured by Swift and Company of Cleveland, OH. The bag measures 43x20 inches. Since this is a seamless bag, it will sell for $34 to $36.

Many textile bags were reused in the feed industry. This 100 pound bag has been reused. It has printing on the outside and on the inside also. The outside has 100 pounds of ARCADY Laying Mash printed on it. The Arcady Farms Milling Company of Chicago, IL manufactured the feed. On the inside of the bag there is printed, PEOPLES Feed. The feed was manufactured by Peoples Supply of Charles Town, WV. This bag measures 38x22 inches. It will sell for $30 to $32.

The feed sacks were one of the most popular ways to clothe the American family and decorate the rural American home during the first half of the twentieth century. Millions of feed sacks were manufactured during this time, but so many were recycled that they are hard to find. Especially hard to find are the print sacks with the labels still on them. The textile feed bags are certainly an exciting collection area today.

### TEXTILE FEED BAGS NOT PICTURED

100 pound white feed textile bag that held MASTER MIX Laying Mash. The McMillen Feed Mills of Fort Wayne, IN milled the feed. The bag measures 38x22 inches ..................... $24 to $26

100 pound white textile feed bag that held TI-O-GA Quality Feed. The Tioga Mills, Inc. of Waverly, NY milled the feed. The Werthan Bag Corp. of Nashville manufactured the bag that measures 22x40 inches or 3.75 yard ............................. $18 to $20

100 pound white textile feed bag that held MOGUL Corn. The Corn Products Refining Co. of New York manufactured the feed. The bag measures 38x20 inches ........................... $12 to $14

100 pound white with green printing textile feed bag that held VITALITY Starter Grower. The Vitality Mills, Inc. of Chicago, IL milled the feed. The bag has a well printed house scene on the front. The bag measures 38x20 inches .................... $20 to $22

100 pound white textile feed bag that held G.L.F. Quality Feed. The feed was milled by Coop. G.L.F. Mills, Inc. of Buffalo, NY. The bag measures 39x20 inches ............................ $14 to $16

# CHAPTER 6

## THE SEAMLESS A BAGS AND TEXTILE SEED BAGS

The farmer not only carried his feed home in the textile bags; he also carried his seed home in the cotton textile bags. Bags from the small 5 pounder to the 2½ bushel seamless bags were used. The seed industry used about 10% of the textile bags produced. The seamless textile bags were used extensively in the seed industry. The seamless 2 bushel bag measuring 45x20 inches was a popular size. Other sizes of seamless bags used were the 1 bushel size measuring 30x18 inches, the 2½ bushel size measuring 48x20 inches and the 100 pound size measuring 36x19 inches.

The seed companies started to buy good toweling bags in the late 1920's in an endeavor to obtain a package that would be consumed, utilized and attractive to the housewife.

The textile cotton seed bags were usually made of osnaburg which is a coarse yarn, of low count, good strength, low cost and able to serve as a multiple trip container. The seamless A seed bags and the plain seed bags will be discussed in this chapter.

The seamless A bags were used mostly for grain and seed. These bags began carrying crops to market in the early 1900's. The seamless A bags quickly became the "seed bag" of America. The seamless A bags are woven on tubular weaving looms to form a tube or bag without the seam.

The Bemis Brother Bag Company made its first Bemis A Seamless in 1909. This company produced and sold 500,000 to 750,000 seamless A bags in 1959. 25 years earlier, they were producing 2 to 3 million seamless A bags each year.

The following companies manufactured the seamless A bags: Ames Bag Company, Anchor Bag Company, Beco Bag Company, Bemis Brother Bag Company, Chase Bag Company, Cincinnati Bag Company, Fulton Bag Company, Ohio Bag Company, Samson Bag Company, Scottsdale Mills, Royal River Seamless and Wagbag. Since just a few companies manufactured these seamless A bags, they are hard to find. When the collector does find a seamless A bag, it may not be in good condition and many bags will be patched because the bags were used over and over.

There was a junior size seamless A bag produced also. This junior size bag measured about 36x20 inches and was used both in the flour and seed industries. There were very few of these junior size seamless A bags produced as compared to the seamless A regular bags. When the collector does find a junior size seamless A bag, it is a rare find.

On the following pages, there are pictures, descriptions and a price guide for the junior size seamless A bags, regular size seamless A bags and the plain, seamed seed bags.

Picture courtesy of
Russell W. Carpenter

This FULTON Seamless A Junior size textile bag held 98 pounds at one time. This white bag has the red and blue stripes on the side of the bag. This bag was manufactured by Fulton Bag Co. and measures 36x20 inches. Since this bag is a rare size and has the beautiful eagle on the front, it will sell for $75 to $80.

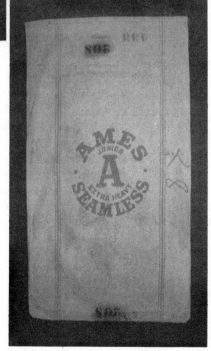

This is an AMES Junior size extra heavy Seamless A bag. There are red stripes on each side. This bag was manufactured by the Ames Bag Co. and measures 34x19 inches. This bag is in excellent condition and a rare size. It will sell for $68 to $70.

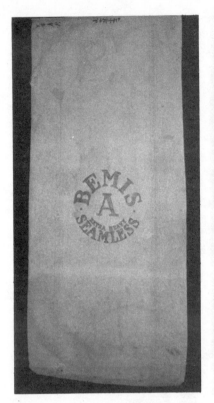 

These two bags are both the famous BEMIS extra heavy seamless A bags. They were manufactured by the Bemis Brother Bag Co. The bags both held 2 bushels of seed and measure 45x20 inches. These bags are in excellent condition with the red and blue stripes down the side. They will sell for $66 to $68.

This is a CHASE extra quality Seamless A cotton textile bag. The bag was manufactured by the Chase Bag Company. The bag measures 42x18½ inches and held 2 bushels of seed. This bag will sell for $40 to $42.

This Triple B Seamless cotton textile bag measures 41x19 inches. The red and blue stripes run along each side of this seamless bag that held 2 bushels of seed at one time. This bag will sell for $30 to $32.

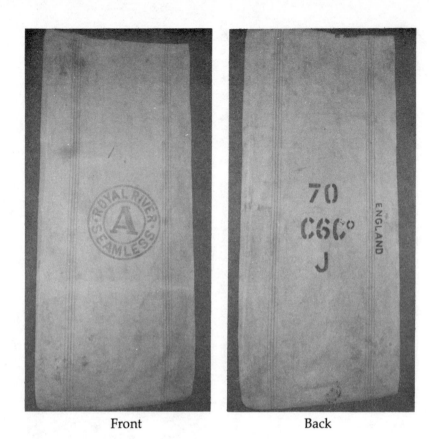

Front                                    Back

This 2 bushel ROYAL RIVER Seamless A bag was manufactured by
Scottdale Mills of Scottdale, GA. This bag was used as an export bag
to England at one time. The bag measures 45x20 inches and will sell
for $30 to $32.

 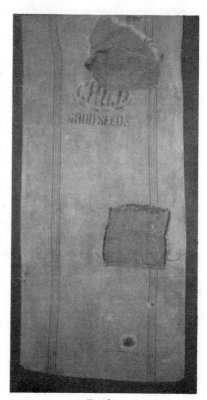

Front        Back

This is a CINCINNATI Seamless A bag and has been used as a multi-trip bag because it is well worn and patched. 2 bushels of Child Good Seeds came in the bag at one time. The seamless bag measures 43x20 inches and was manufactured by the Cincinnati Bag Company. The bag will sell for $30 to $32.

This SAMSON A Extra Heavy seamless textile seed bag was manufactured by the Samson Bag Company. It measures 43x19 inches and has the red and blue stripes down the sides. This bag held 2 bushels of seed at one time. It will sell for $30 to $32.

This OHIO Seamless A bag was manufactured by the Ohio Bag Company. The bag has red stripes down each side and measures 45x20 inches. This seamless A bag will sell for $30 to $32.

This ANCHOR Seamless A bag held 2 bushels of seed. The bag was manufactured by the Anchor Bag Company. The bag has red and blue stripes on each side and measures 44x21 inches. This bag will sell for $30 to $32.

This BOOTT Seamless A bag is not in very good condition, but it shows another company that manufactured the seamless A bags. The bag had the red and blue stripes down each side and measures 43x19 inches. This bag will sell for $12 to $14.

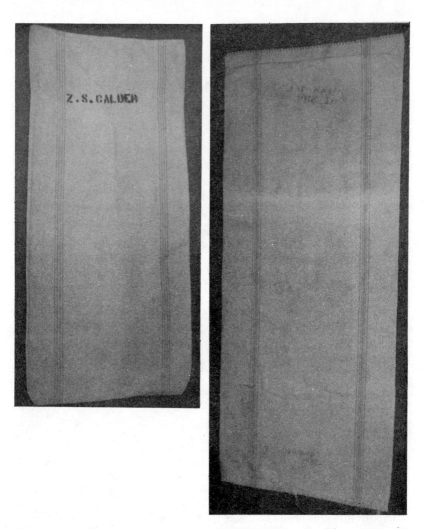

These two seamless bags measure 45x20 inches each. They both held about 2 bushels of seed. Both bags have the red and blue stripes down the side. Since these bags have no printing on them, they will sell for $18 to $20.

Photo courtesy of Russell W. Carpenter Garst and Thomas Hybrid Grain Sorghum seed came in this textile bag. There were only a few cotton textile bags manufactured with the Garst and Thomas name on them. Garst and Thomas developed the hybrid sorghum seed at the time paper bags were becoming popular, so just a few seeds were packaged in the textile bags. Garst and Thomas Hybrid Corn Co. of Coon Rapids, IA produced the seed. The bag was manufactured by Chase Bag Co. of St. Louis. The bag measures 15½x9½ inches. This bag, because it is rare, will sell for $34 to $36.

BELL'S BRAND SEEDS came in this white cotton textile bag. The American Seed Co. of Forth Worth, TX produced the seed. The bag was manufactured by Fulton Bags of Dallas. The bag measures 24x14 inches. This well printed bag will sell for $20 to $22.

One bushel of PLOWMAN SEED came in this white cotton textile bag. The seed was produced by W.L. Crawford Seed Co. of Mayfield, KY. The bag was manufactured by the Werthan Bag Co. of Nashville, TN. The bag measures 29x16 inches. This beautifully printed bag will sell for $30 to $32.

This white, well printed, textile bag held MONUMENT Quality Field Seed at one time. The seeds were produced by the Wayne Feed Supply Co., Inc. of Arthur, IL. The bag measures 32x16 inches and will sell for $18 to $20.

ASGROW Vegetable seeds came in this textile bag. The seeds were grown by Associated Seed Growers, Inc. The bag, manufactured by Bemis Bag Company, measures 38x17 inches and will sell for $16 to $18.

OKLAHOMA Approved Alfalfa Winter Hardy seed came in this white textile bag. The seed were produced under the supervision of Oklahoma Crop Improvement Ass'n. of Stillwater, OK. The bag was manufactured by Bemis Bag Co. This bag measures 25x15 inches and will sell for $12 to $14.

60 pounds of BUFFALO Alfalfa Seed came in this white textile bag. The bag measures 28x14½ inches and will sell for $24 to $26.

RANGER ALFALFA Seed came in this white textile bag. The seed were produced by Nafco-Portland. This bag measures 30x15 inches and will sell for $12 to $14.

60 pounds of DAKOTA COM-MON ALFALFA Seed came in this textile bag. There is no seed manufacturer printed on the bag. This bag measures 30x15 inches and will sell for $12 to $14.

One bushel or 56 pounds of PFISTER HYBRIDS Seed Corn came in this textile bag. Pfister Associated Growers, Inc. produced the seed. Werthan Bag Company of Nashville, TN manufactured the bag. This bag measures 30x16½ inches. This bag will sell for $16 to $18.

Seed corn is one of the most common found seed bags today. There were so many brands produced. This picture shows another sack collector, Russell W. Carpenter of Iowa, with his seed bag collection.

Picture courtesy of
Le Spearman of Iowa

One bushel or 56 pounds of
CLOVER HILL Hybrid Seed
Corn came in this textile bag.
Clover Hill Hybrid Seed Corn Co.
of Audubon, IA produced the
seed. The bag was manufactured
by Hutchinson Bag Corp. of Hutchinson, KS. This bag measures
32x17 inches and will sell for $12
to $14.

Picture and bag courtesy of
Laura Mize of St. Louis, Missouri

Diamond Quality MAGEE
Hybrids Seed Corn came in this
well printed bag. The seed were
produced by the Magee Seed
Company of Bloomfield, MO.
Semmes Bag Co. of Memphis,
TN manufactured the bag. This
bag measures 31x17 inches and
will sell for $20 to $22.

109

One bushel of MACON Hybrid Seed Corn came in this white, cotton textile bag. The seeds were produced by the Macon Seed Company, Inc. of Decatur, IL. The bag was manufactured by Fulton Bag Company. This bag measures 31x15 inches and will sell for $24 to $26.

BURRUS Quality Hybrid Corn Seed came in this cotton textile bag. The corn seed was produced by Burrus Bros. and Associated Growers of Arenzville, IL. This seed bag measures 31x15 inches. This bag will sell for $18 to $20.

110

One bushel or 56 pounds of DEKALB Seed Corn came in both these textile bags. Dekalb Agricultural Association, Inc. of Dekalb, IL produced the seed. The bag pictured on the left is a Duotex Type Bemis Waterproof Bag and was manufactured by Bemis Brother Bag Co. of St. Louis. This bag measures 30x18 inches. The second bag pictured is a waterproof bag that measures 31x15½ inches. Dekalb has been producing seed corn since 1917. These bags will sell for $26 to $28 each.

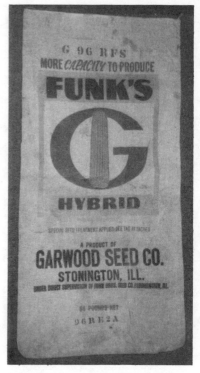

FUNK'S Hybrid G Seed Corn came in both these bags. One bushel of COLUMBIANA FUNK'S Hybrid G seed corn came in the bag on the left. The seed was produced by the Columbiana Seed Co. of Eldred, IL. Bemis Brother Bag Co. of St. Louis manufactured the bag. The bag measures 29x16 inches and is well printed on both sides. The bag on the right held 56 pounds of FUNK'S Hybrid seed corn produced by Garwood Seed Co. of Stonington, IL. This waterproof bag measures 31x15 inches. The bags will sell for $18 to $20.

CANTERBURY Hybrid seed corn produced by C.E. Canterbury Seed Co. of Sangamon County, Cantrall, IL came in this textile bag. The bag was manufactured by Fulton and measures 31x15 inches. This bag will sell for $18 to $20.

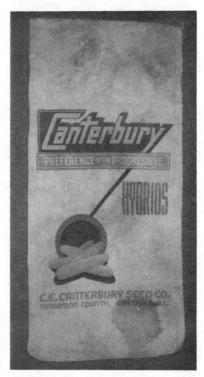

One bushel of RUBY GREEN Clover seed came in this white textile bag. The seeds were produced by the Ruby Green Inc. seed house of Kirksville, MO. The 30x14 inch bag was manufactured by the Werthan Bag Corp. of Nashville, TN. This bag will sell for $20 to $22.

50 pounds of YUCHI Certified Clover Seed produced by the Central Alabama Certified Seed Producers Ass'n of Prattville, AL came in this white cotton textile bag. The bag measures 30x14½ inches and will sell for $16 to $18.

One bushel of GRO-COATED Red Clover seed came in this white textile bag. The bag measures 30x15 inches and is well printed on both sides. This bag will sell for $16 to $18.

100 pounds of DELTAPINE 15 Cotton Seed came in this textile bag. The seeds were produced in 1950 by Delta and Pine Land Co. of Scott, MS. The Deltapine cotton seed varieties were popular because of their high yield per acre, the ease with which they clean at the gins and their comparative strength. They were developed in the Mississippi Delta but are now used all across the Cotton Belt. This bag was manufactured by Fulton Bags of New Orleans. The bag measures 38x23 inches. This bag will sell for $24 to $26.

Picture courtesy of Monnie Cook

100 pounds of RATIO Certified Quality Cotton Seed came in this cotton textile bag. Peter and Griffin of Ratio, AR produced the seed. The bag measures 37½x22 inches. This bag will sell for $12 to $14.

100 pounds of BROME GRASS Seed came in this 39x26 white cotton textile bag. This bag will sell for $14 to $16.

100 pounds of BLUE SEAL seeds came in this white cotton textile bag. The seed were produced by the Illinois Farm Supply Company of Chicago, IL. Bemis-St. Louis manufactured the bag. The bag measures 38x22 inches and will sell for $20 to $22.

Most seed bags came with certification tags on them. The tabs were usually discarded when the seed were used. The tags pictured show the type of tags that came on one bag of seed. One tag shows the purity guarantee with a state stamp on it. One shows that the seed have been treated with poison. The last one shows the seed were Mississippi registered cotton planting seed.

The seamed textile bags that held seed in the past can be found with relative ease. The seamless A bags are harder to find, but there are still some out there. Consider youself lucky if you come across a regular seamless A bag, but if you were to find a junior size seamless A bag consider yourself blessed.

Seeds can still be purchased in the textile bags today, but most seeds are packaged in the multiwall paper bags.

### TEXTILE SEED BAGS NOT PICTURED

100 pound white textile Seamless A bag that held seeds. The bag is marked USS 22 Baltimore Product of The Netherlands. This bag measures 42x18 inches. This was an import bag at one time.
. . . . . . . . . . . . . . . . . . . . . . . . . . . . . . . . . . . . . . . . . . . . . . . . . . . . . . $24 to $26

A white textile bag that held one bushel of Tennessee Certified Hybrid Seed Corn. The seed was certified by the Tennessee Corp. Improvement Ass'n. The bag was DDT treated when the seeds were packaged. The bag measures 35x13 inches. . . . . . . . . . . . . . . . . . . . . $12 to $14

50 pound white textile bag that held REGAL Certified Ladino Clover Seed. The bag measures 29½x12 inches. . . . . . . . . . . . . . $12 to $14

100 pound white textile bag that held PARK Lawn Seed Mixture. The seed was packed by L. Teweles Seed Co. of Milwaukee, WI. Chase Bag Co. manufactured the bag. . . . . . . . . . . . . . . . . . . . . . $14 to $16

A white textile bag that held one bushel of Quality Deep Grain Hybrid Seed Corn. Mo-Ark Co. of Hayti, MO produced the seed.
. . . . . . . . . . . . . . . . . . . . . . . . . . . . . . . . . . . . . . . . . . . . . . . . . . . . . . $10 to $12

A white cotton textile bag that held KANSAS Hardy Alfalfa Seed. The bag was manufactured by Central Bag Co. of Kansas City, MO. This bag has a beautiful picture of the U.S.A. with a heart in the center. . . . . . . . . . . . . . . . . . . . . . . . . . . . . . . . . . . . . . . . . . . . . $18 to $20

25 pound cream colored textile bag that held SHADY NOOK Mixed Lawn Seed. Cadwell & Jones, Inc. of East Hartford, CT produced the seed. This bag measures 29x17½ inches. . . . . . . . . . . . . . $18 to $20

# CHAPTER 7

## SPECIALTY PRODUCTS AND TEXTILE BAGS

Specialty textile bags made up about 19% of the total textile bag production. Specialty bags packaged almost every item that the housewife could buy and bring home to use. Some of these include meal, salt, coffee, meats, rice, peanuts, soap flakes, bath crystals, peas, beans, and starch. The farmer or man of the house could bring home products like tobacco, fertilizer, mulch, cement, tire chains or lead shot packaged in cotton textile bags. This specialty group of textile bags also included the textile mailer bag, the sample bag, the money bags and the cotton pick sacks. There were not as many of these specialty bags produced as there were of flour, sugar, feed and seed so they are rarer. The following pages describe many of the specialty bags mentioned above, feature pictures of the bags and give a price guide for the collector.

Meats such as bacon, sausage and ham came in the white cotton textile bags.

 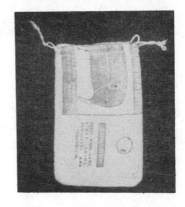

Front                                              Back

One pound of Whole Hog Sausage came in this small textile bag. Archie McFarland and Son of South Salt Lake, UT produced the sausage. Someone over the years has added the drawstring to the bag so that it could be used for storage. The bag measures 6x3½ inches and will sell for $5 to $7.

Front                                    Back

Luter's Genuine Smithfield Bacon came in this cotton textile bag. The Smithfield Packing Co., Inc. of Smithfield, VA, a subsidiary of Smithfield Foods, Inc. manufactured the bacon. The bag measures 12x8 inches. This bag has cooking directions printed on the back. The bag will sell for $10 to $12.

25 pounds of LOTUS Long Grain Rice came in this white cotton textile bag. Riceland Foods of Stuttgart, AR produced the rice. Someone has embroidered over the printing on the bag making this bag a colorful work of art. The bag measures 19x14 inches and will sell for $16 to $18.

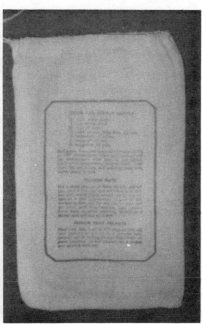

| Front | Back |

Three pounds of GOLD KIST raw shelled peanuts came in this white cotton textile bag. The Gold Kist Peanuts division of Gold Kist Inc. of Atlanta, GA manufactured the peanuts. The back of this bag is printed with three recipes. This bag measures 10½x7 inches and will sell for $10 to $12.

CANILLA Brand Extra Fancy Long Grain Rice came in this white cotton textile bag. The bag was manufactured by the Langston Bag Co. of Memphis, TN. The bag measures 15x10 inches. This well printed rice bag will sell for $12 to $14.

Corn meal was packaged in 5, 10, 25, 50 or 100 pound bags. The meal industry used about 2.8% of the total textile bags produced. Many skillets of brown crusty corn bread was baked using the corn meal that came in these textile bags. This picture shows the skillet and corn bread stick pans that were used to make corn bread.

25 pounds of RED HEAD white corn meal came in this white cotton textile bag. The meal was manufactured by Shreveport Grain and Elev. Co. of Shreveport, LA. The bag was manufactured by the Central Bag Co. of Kansas City, MO. The bag measures 26x13 inches. This colorful bag will sell for $30 to $32.

100 pounds of Choice Recleaned MICHIGAN NAVY BEANS came in this white textile bag. McLaughlin Ward and Co. of Jackson, MI packaged the beans. The bag was manufactured by Bader Bros. Bag Co. This bag measures 34x16 inches and will sell for $12 to $14.

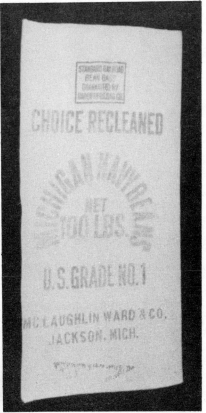

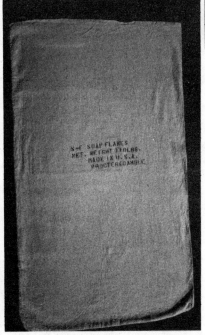

110 pounds of Soap Flakes came in this white textile bag. Procter and Gamble manufactured the soap flakes. Procter and Gamble was founded in 1837 by William Procter and James Gamble. This bag measures 38x23 inches and will sell for $18 to $20.

3 pounds of SCHRATZ Bath Crystals water softener came in this white textile bag. The Schratz Co., founded in 1868, manufactured the bath crystals. This bag measures 13x5½ inches and will sell for $10 to $12.

25 pounds of Roasted COFFEE came in this white textile bag manufactured by Fulton Bags of St. Louis. The bag measures 28x17 inches and will sell for $20 to $22.

Coffee came in textile bags ranging in sizes from the small ½ pound bag to the large 150 pound import bags.

Front                                        Back

Picture courtesy of Monta Jean and Weldon Evans

One pound of TEXIN Coffee came in this small textile bag. This coffee was processed, selected, roasted, ground and packed by Cafes Texin of Veracruz, Mexico. This bag measures 9½x6½ inches and will sell for $6 to $8.

This white cotton textile bag was used as an import bag for coffee. 150 pounds of clean coffee came in the bag. This coffee was imported from Guatemala in 1944 - 1945. This bag measures 39x25 inches and will sell for $30 to $32.

The white cotton textile bags were used to ship coffee samples in. Sometimes these samples were shipped from the coffee plantations. Three of these sample mailer bags are included here.

This coffee sample bag was sent from Gulf Atlantic Warehouse Co.., Houston Wharf Co. of Houston, TX. The bag measures 10½x5 inches and will sell for $8 to $10.

This white textile bag was used for shipping sample coffee. The address, From J. A. Folger and Co., Box 456, Kansas City 10, Missouri, was printed on the bag. The bag measures 15x8 inches and will sell for $8 to $10.

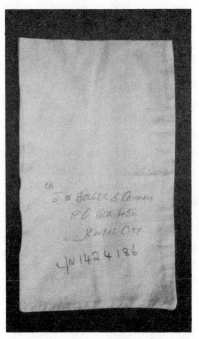

This white textile bag was used to mail sample coffee to J.A. Folger and Company, P. O. Box 456, Kansas City, MO. This sample was mailed from Halli Brothers Limited, Box 9794, Nairobi. This bag measures 15x9 inches and will sell for $16 to $18.

Salt was usually shipped either in bulk or barrels until the 1900's. After that, some cloth bags were used for packaging salt. The salt industry used only a very small percent of the cotton textile bags that were manufactured so they are harder to find than other bags.

Three pounds of WORCESTER SALT came in this white textile bag. Their slogan was "It Takes The Best To Make The Best." The Worcester SAlt Co. of New York, NY manufactured the salt. The refinery was located at Silver Springs, NY. An elephant head was printed on the bag. The bag measures 10x5½ inches and will sell for $12 to $14.

Four pounds of MORTON Table Salt came in this textile bag. The salt was manufactured by the Morton Salt Company of Chicago, IL. Morton Salt Co. was established in 1848 in Chicago. Today, Morton Salt is the world's leading producer and marketer of salt for the home, food service, industrial, agricultural and highway use. This well printed bag measures 12x6 inches. This bag will sell for $12 to $14.

Three pounds of CHIPPEWA Table Salt manufactured by Ohio Salt Co. of Wadsworth, OH came in this white textile bag. The Ohio Salt Co. was founded in 1898 by E.J. Young and became part of Morton Salt Division in 1948. This bag has printing on both sides and measures 11x5½ inches. The bag will sell for $14 to $16.

Ten pounds of CHIPPEWA Salt for general purposes came in this white cotton textile bag. The Ohio Salt Co. of Wadsworth, OH manufactured the salt. This bag has the Indian head on both sides. The bag measures 14x8 inches and will sell for $16 to $18.

50 pounds of CHIPPEWA Medium Salt came in this cotton textile bag. The salt was manufactured by The Ohio Salt Co. of Wadsworth, OH which was established in 1898 by E.J. Young and purchased by Morton Salt Division in 1948. The bag measures 28x14½ inches. With the well printed Indian head, this bag will sell for $40 to $44.

100 pounds of CHIPPEWA Kiln Dried Granulated Salt came in this white textile bag. The salt was manufactured by The Ohio Salt Co. of Wadsworth, OH. This well printed bag measures 29x15 inches and will sell for $40 to $44.

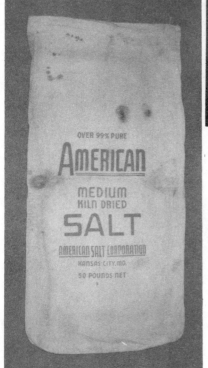

50 pounds of AMERICAN Salt came in this white textile bag. The salt was manufactured by the American Salt Corporation of Kansas City, MO. The bag measures 29x14 inches and will sell for $14 to $16.

56 pounds of CRESCENT Salt came in this white cotton textile bag. The salt was manufactured by The Colonial Salt Co. of Akron, OH. This bag measures 30x14 inches. This well printed bag will sell for $24 to $26.

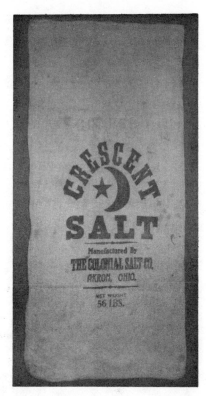

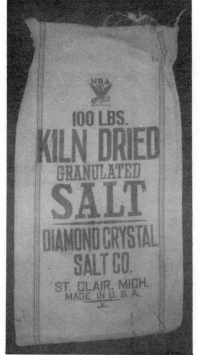

100 pounds of DIAMOND CRYSTAL Salt came in this textile bag. The kiln dried salt was manufactured by the Diamond Crystal Salt Co. of St. Clair, MI. The bag measures 30x17 inches and will sell for $20 to $22.

100 pounds of JEFFERSON ISLAND Salt came in this white cotton textile bag. The salt was distributed by Jefferson Island Salt Co. of Louisville, KY. I can remember when Jefferson Island Salt was a sponsor for part of the Grand Ole Opry on radio years ago. This bag measures 29x17 inches and will sell for $14 to $16.

This small U.S. MAIL cotton textile bag was mailed from California to Tennessee. It cost 1½¢ to mail the bag. The bag measures 3x2½ inches and will sell for $20 to $22.

132

Tobacco for pipes and cigarettes came in these four small white textile bags. "COUNTRY GENTLEMAN" tobacco by the Myers Tobacco Co. of Durham, NC came in the first bag. The second held OUR ADVERTISER tobacco by R.J. Reynolds Tobacco Co. of Winston-Salem, NC. OLD HILL SIDE tobacco by R.C. Owen Co. of Gallatin, TN came in the third bag. The last bag held ORPHAN BOY tobacco by John Weisert Tobacco Co. of St. Louis, MO. The bags measure 5x3 inches and will sell for $6 to $9.

This small cotton sample textile bag was used by the H.C. Cole Milling Co. of Chester, IL. This company was established in 1839. The bag measures 13x7½ inches and will sell for $10 to $12.

133

This small cotton textile mailer bag was used by the Dixie-Portland Flour Mills, Inc. of Arkansas City, KS to mail samples. This bag measures 17x10 inches and will sell for $10 to $12.

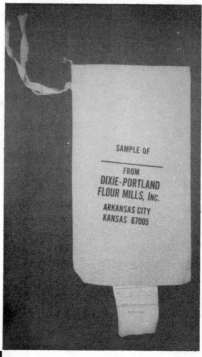

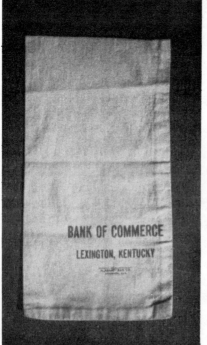

This is a cotton textile money bag that was manufactured by the Alabama Bag Co. of Anniston, AL. The bag was used by the Bank of Commerce of Lexington, KY. The bag measures 14½x8 inches and will sell for $10 to $12.

This is a cotton textile money bag. The printing on the bag states 'Return This Sack to Federal Reserve Bank of Kansas City, Missouri 2'. The bag measures 12x7 inches and will sell for $10 to $12.

25 pounds of LAWRENCE Lead Shot came in this textile bag. The shot was manufactured by the National Lead Company of St. Louis, MO. The bag measures 14x6 inches and will sell for $6 to $8.

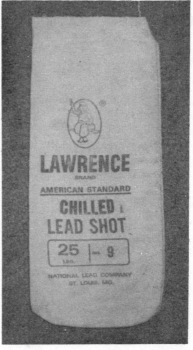

Back

Front

Picture courtesy of Charlotte Watson Knight.

25 pounds of HAPPY DOG FOOD came in this well printed white textile bag. The dog food was manufactured by Happy Mills of Memphis, TN. Bemis Bags manufactured the bag. The bag measures 25x13 inches and will sell for $18 to $20.

McKAY Tire Chains for a passenger car came in this cotton textile bag. The tire chains were manufactured by The McKay Company of Pittsburg, PA. The bag measures 16x10 inches. This bag will sell for $18 to $20.

94 pounds of MARQUETTE CEMENT came in this textile bag. The cement was manufactured by the Marquette Cement Manufacturing Co. of Chicago and Memphis with plants at La Salle, IL and Cape Girardiau, MO. Bemis Brother Bag Co. manufactured the bag. The bag measures 29x16 inches and will sell for $12 to $14.

Cement came in the cotton textile bags. Today, regular cement is the only product still sold in bag sizes to correspond with barrel measurements. A barrel of cement weighs 376 pounds. Bags of regular cement are sometimes sold in the ¼ barrel size of 94 pounds.

100 pounds of MEX-R-CO FIRE CLAY came in this white textile bag. Mexico Refractories Co. of Mexico, MO manufactured this fire clay. The bag measures 30x16 inches and will sell for $10 to $12.

100 pounds of FUZZY MULCH came in this white cotton textile bag. The bag has a picture of Colonel "SCO-CO" on the bag. The mulch was manufactured by the Southern Cotton Oil Division, Hunt Foods and Industries, Inc. of Memphis, TN. The bag was manufactured by Langston Bags of Memphis and measures 39x27 inches. This well printed bag will sell for $22 to $24.

Fertilizer was also purchased by the farmer in the white cotton textile bags. Fertilizer used about .6% of the total textile bags produced.

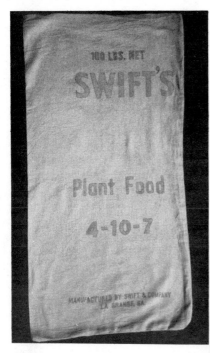

100 pounds of SWIFT'S 4-10-7 plant food came in this white cotton textile bag. The fertilizer was manufactured by Swift and Company of La Grange, GA. The bag measures 34x18 inches and will sell for $10 to $12.

100 pounds of ROYSTER GUANO Fertilizer came in this cotton textile bag. The F.S. Royster Guano Co. of Jackson, MS manufactured the fertilizer. The bag measures 34x17 inches and will sell for $12 to $14.

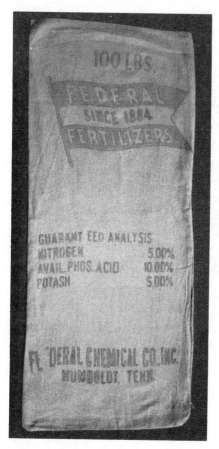

100 pounds of FEDERAL FERTI-LIZER came in this cotton textile bag. Federal Chemical Co. of Humboldt, TN manufactured the fertilizer. This company was established in 1884. The bag measures 36x16 inches and will sell for $14 to $16.

All cotton was picked by hand until 1936 when the first mechanical cotton picker came out. Even after the mechanical picker was on the market, cotton was still picked by hand. The individual that picked the cotton pulled a cotton pick sack, the largest cotton textile bag made. It had a strap that went over the picker's shoulder. The cotton pick sacks have been pulled countless miles up and down the cotton rows. These sacks were made of 30 inch osnaburg or 8 to 12 ounce duck and came in several lengths. Some of these different lengths were the 6, 7, 7½, 8, 9, 10 and the longer 12 foot lengths. The smaller pick sacks were usually used by children. When pickers could not afford to buy a pick sack, they would make their own pick sacks. Sometimes these homemade cotton pick sacks were made by using the feed and seed textile bags.

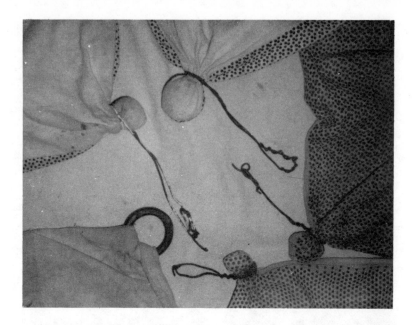

The cotton pick sacks needed to be weighed when the picker had his sack full. To help hold the sack on the hook where it could be weighed, a hanger was put on one of the lower corners of the pick sack. These hangers were made from wire, coat hangers, large washers, etc. A green cotton boll was put inside the corner of the sack, then the hanger was tied around the green boll. The picture shows some of the homemade hangers added to the pick sacks. Later the bag manufacturers began to add a grommet in the lower corner of the cotton pick sack.

The first cotton pick sacks were made without a protective coating on the bottom. Later the bag manufacturers began to add a tar coating to the bottom of the bags. When plastic became popular, a coating of plastic dots was added to the bottom of the pick sacks. This made the cotton sack last longer. The following pictures show some cotton pick sacks.

This 9 foot BEMIS Extra Quality cotton pick sack was manufactured by the Bemis Brother Bag Company. The pick sack has no coating on the bottom. This sack is 9 feet long, 27 inches wide and made of 9.93 oz. duck. This pick sack will sell for $30 to $34.

This is a 4 foot Bemis Asphalt Bottom Extra Heavy cotton pick sack. Asphalt was added to the bottom to make the sack last longer. The advertising for the Bemis Asphalt Bottom cotton pick sack was in *The Arkansas Farmer,* October 1949 issue. This bag will sell for $40 to $45.

INSIST ON **BEMIS**
**ASPHALT BOTTOM**
**COTTON PICK SACKS**

THE LONGEST WEARING COTTON PICK SACK
ON THE MARKET.    OUTLASTS TWO OR
THREE DUCK BAGS – BY ACTUAL TEST.
THE ASPHALT BOTTOM WEARS LIKE IRON.

*Manufactured By*
**BEMIS BRO. BAG CO.**
MEMPHIS 2, TENN.

**For Sale By ALL LEADING JOBBERS**

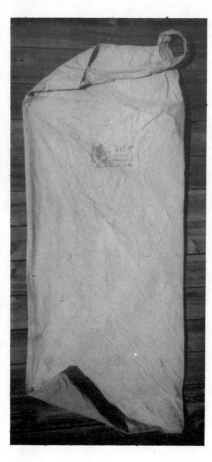

This is a 6 foot BEMIS DURA-DOT cotton pick sack. The bag was manufactured by Bemis Brother Bag Company. It has the black plastic dots on the bottom. This sack is 6 feet long and 27 inches wide. This cotton pick sack will sell for $26 to $28.

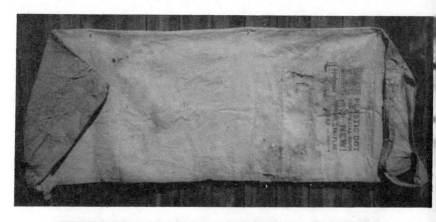

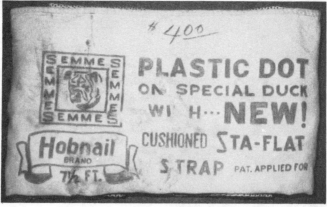

This 7½ foot HOBNAIL Brand Plasti Dot cotton pick sack had a New Cushioned Sta-Flat strap. The cotton pick sack cost $4.00 when new and was manufactured by Semmes Bag Co. of Memphis, TN. This 26 inch wide sack has black plastic dots on the bottom and will sell for $28 to $30.

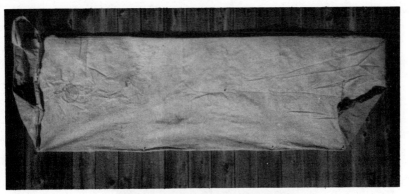

This is a 9 foot PANTHER Brand Plastic Dot All Duck cotton pick sack. The sack is 27 inches wide and has black plastic dots on the bottom. This sack will sell for $32 to $34.

The collector of specialty textile bags will have the thrill of finding unusual bags that packaged products in the early 1900's. The ones mentioned in this chapter are a sample not a complete listing. These specialty bags are especially nice to display in the kitchen.

## TEXTILE SPECIALTY BAGS NOT PICTURED

4 pound white textile bag that held table salt. Table salt is printed on the front in green lettering. The bag measures 11x5½ inches.
. . . . . . . . . . . . . . . . . . . . . . . . . . . . . . . . . . . . . . . . . . . . . . . . . . . . . . $4 to $6

100 pound white textile bag that held KOSHER Salt. The salt was manufactured by Wadsworth Salt Co. of Wadsworth, OH. Chase Bag Co. manufactured the bag that measures 36x16½ inches.
. . . . . . . . . . . . . . . . . . . . . . . . . . . . . . . . . . . . . . . . . . . . . . . . . . . . . $18 to $20

A white textile commercial laundry bag that measures 34x25 inches. The commercial laundry bag was used by Independence Laundry and Cleaning Co. . . . . . . . . . . . . . . . . . . . . . . . . . . . . . . . . . . . . . . $6 to $8

A 9 foot Bemis Dura-Dot cotton pick sack. The sack was manufactured by Bemis Brother Bag Co. The sack has blue plastic dots on the bottom and cost $3.25 when new. The sack is 9 feet long and 27 inches wide. . . . . . . . . . . . . . . . . . . . . . . . . . . . . . . . . . . . . . . . . . . $26 to $28

A 2 in 1 RIEGEL "Plastic-Dot" 10½ foot cotton pick sack. This sack was unusual because it had plastic dots on both sides of the sack and a strap that could be changed from one side to the other. This cotton pick sack could be used on one side until it wore thin then turned over and used on the other. It lasted longer. The sack was 10½ feet long and 27 inches wide. . . . . . . . . . . . . . . . . . . . . . . . . . . . $38 to $40

148

# CHAPTER 8

## CLOTHING MADE FROM THE TEXTILE BAGS

At no time during the period of textiles has the array of colors been more spectacular than those of the textile bag era. The colors were many and the patterns were endless. This was what made the material from these bags so desirable to the housewife of the 1920's, 1930's, 1940's and 1950's. The lady of the house clothed her family in the material from these bags. She made dresses, shirts, blouses, skirts, pants, shorts, coats, jackets, aprons and almost every item of clothing for family members. She used the white textile bags for making diapers for the babies, panties, slips, gowns, pajamas, shorts and before the day of the store-bought sanitary napkins, she folded the white cotton textile bags into sanitary napkins. The ladies of a community would exchange print bags so they could get several bags of a matching print or pattern to make items of clothing.

The cotton textile bags in which sugar, salt, flour, feed, seeds, fertilizer and meal came in were all used. These bags came in white, prints and colors. The fabrics were colorfast, washable, durable, 100% cotton and available in a wide range of colors and designs. No bag was too small to be used. If a housewife needed more bags, she could purchase bags for a few cents from almost any baker, grocer, mail order house or large department store. The following bag sizes and yardage was published by the National Cotton Council of Memphis, Tennessee.

| FEED BAGS | FLOUR BAGS | SUGAR BAGS |
|---|---|---|
| 50 lb. 34x38½ | 5 lb. 15x19 | 5 lb. 13x16 |
| 100 lb. 39x46 | 10 lb. 18x23 | 10 lb. 16x21 |
| 39x48 | 25 lb. 26x26 | 25 lb. 22x27 |
| 39x50 | 50 lb. 30x34 | 100 lb. 36x40 |
| 39x52 | 100 lb. 36x42 | |
| 39x54 | | |

| SALT BAGS | MEAL BAGS | FERTILIZER BAGS |
|---|---|---|
| 5 lb. 13x14 | 5 lb. 15x16 | 100 lb. 36x39 |
| 10 lb. 16x17 | 10 lb. 18x22 | 125 lb. 36x45 |
| 25 lb. 18x26 | 25 lb. 26x27 | 150 lb. 39x44 |
| 100 lb. 30x36 | 100 lb. 36x44 | 200 lb. 39x52 |

The National Cotton Council of Memphis, Tennessee sponsored two programs in the 1950's to promote the use of the cotton textile bags. The first one was the "Cotton Bag Loan Wardrobe." The second was the "Cotton Bag Sewing Contest."

The "Cotton Bag Loan Wardrobe" was set up where the Cotton Council would loan wardrobes that contained a collection of 18 attractive fashions featuring McCall's patterns and the print and plain fabrics used to make the textile bags that feed, flour, seed, meal, fertilizer and other staple products came in. There were 24 wardrobes available for loan. Twelve were made from one set of McCall's patterns and twelve from another.

A commentary was prepared and sent with each wardrobe as well as suggested news releases. These wardrobes were loaned to any ladies group, community organization or club interested in promoting the reuse of the cotton textile bags or learning how to make clothes using the cotton textile bags.

"Sew Your Way to Fame and Fortune With Cotton Bags" was the way the 1959 Cotton Bag Sewing Contest was headlined. This contest was sponsored by the National Cotton Council and the Textile Manufacturers Association. Contestants could combine bright ideas, cotton bags and their best sewing know-how to win prizes like electric mixers, toasters, automatic fry pans, washer and dryer, gas range or a week's free vacation in Hollywood. Each contestant would enter the cotton bag sewing contest at one of 49 state or regional fairs. Fair winners at the state level would compete at the national level. This also promoted the reuse of the cotton textile bag.

To prepare the bags for reuse, the housewife would rip the chain-stitched closing apart by clipping the threads at the inside bottom corner and pulling both threads to unravel. Next she would need to remove the paper labels or direct on bag printing. This was done by soaking in warm soapy water. The direct printing was usually done in washout inks but usually required longer and stronger soaking for removal. The housewife might have used the following items when laundering the bags: P and G White Laundry Soap, Crystal White Family Soap, a rub board and tub, a wringer washing machine, liquid bluing and starch. After the bags were washed and ironed, they were ready for reuse by the housewife.

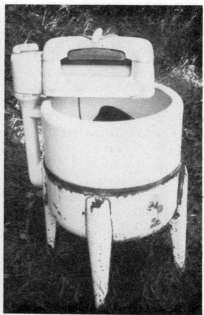

Pictures courtesy of Monnie Cook of Imboden, Arkansas.

The housewife had a great selection of sewing notions to choose from at this time. Patterns, buttons, trim and belt buckles were many and varied. Patterns in these pictures were just a sample of what could be purchased. Patterns at this time sold for 10¢ to 50¢.

Buttons and belt buckles were usually made of pearl or plastic. There was a great variety to choose from. The pictures show a sample of what the housewife could choose from.

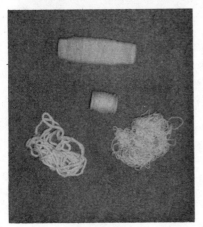

Many housewives not only reused the bag material, they saved the thread that they unraveled from the seams of the bags. This thread was rolled up to be used later. The thread was made of fine cotton and once unraveled, could be used to crochet edgings, doilies, table mats, scarves for tables and many other items. The housewife also used this thread for knitting.

The fine cotton of the textile bags and the thread used to sew them made both these items ideal for tinting or dyeing. Many bags were dyed to match the decor of the home, a color scheme of a hand pieced quilt or a dress ensemble. The picture shows the Putnam Dyes that the housewife might have used.

The following pages feature items and pieces of clothing that were made from the versatile, colorful textile cotton bags of bygone years. A price guide is included for the collector of these colorful items.

This dress for a little girl is blue with white chickens on it. The dress has buttons and trim for the period of the textile bags. This dress dates to the 1940's. The small dresses were usually made with flour sacks. This dress has some rust spots on the shoulders where it has hung on a wire hanger for years. It will sell for $14 to $16.

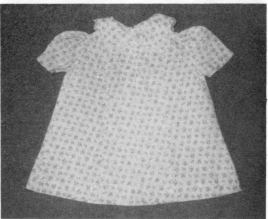

This white dress with blue flowers on it is for a little girl. The dress was made with either a flour or feed textile bag. The dress has white trim on the collar, hand worked buttonholes and little pearl buttons. This dress is from the late 1940's or early 1950's. The dress will sell for $18 to $20.

This white dress with small blue flowers on it was made for a little girl. Fabric from a flour or feed textile bag was used. The dress has white trim around the sleeves, neck and yoke. The dress has hand worked buttonholes and pearl buttons and will sell for $20 to $22.

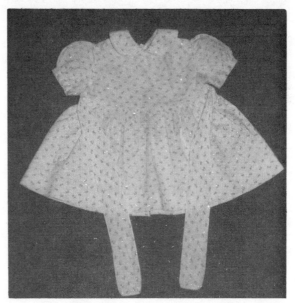

This little girl's white dress with little green cherries on it was made from a feed or flour textile bag. Pink and white trim has been added to the sleeves, collar, waist and hem. The buttonholes have been hand worked. Pearl buttons were used. The dress will sell for $20 to $22.

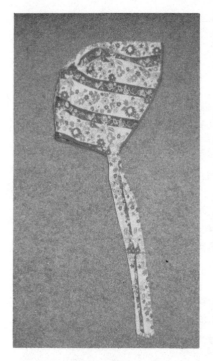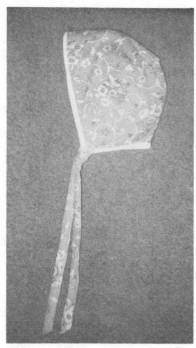

Both of these bonnets were made for a child. Each was made with material from a flour or feed textile bag. The bonnets are both in good condition and will sell for $6 to $8.

This white slip and panties for a little girl were made with the material from the white cotton textile bags. Simplicity pattern number 2558 may have been used. The pattern cost 25¢ when new. The slip and panties will sell for $10 to $12 each.

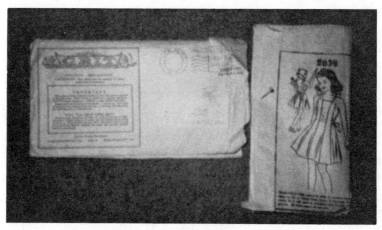

This blue girl's dress with white daisy flowers on it was made from two 100 pound print textile bags. The writing on the material states "He Loves Me" "He Loves Me Not." This dress has white trim and a white tie belt. Pattern number 2638 ordered from GRIT may have been used. The dress will sell for $20 to $22.

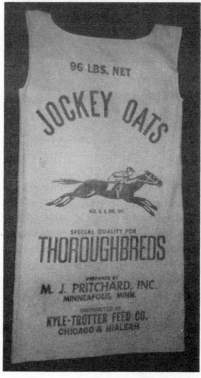

This true sack dress and panties were made from feed sacks. They still have the printing on them. The items were bought at a local flea market. The dress will sell for $20 to $22, the panties $16 to $18 and the sack for $30 to $32.

159

It took two 100 pound print textile feed bags to make these
pajamas for a child. These blue
pajamas with white and dark
blue flowers would be for summer wear; long sleeved pajamas
would be made for winter wear.
These pajamas, with hand
worked buttonholes, are in
excellent condition and will sell
for $16 to $18.

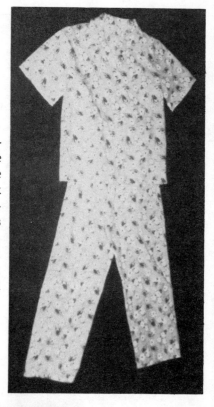

This lady's two-piece
dress was made with
three 100 pound cot-
ton feed bags. This
dress, with blue
flowers, has been
trimmed with white
trim and small bright
blue buttons. The
dress has some fading
across the back, but
the condition is still
good. This dress, with
hand worked button-
holes, will sell for $20
to $24.

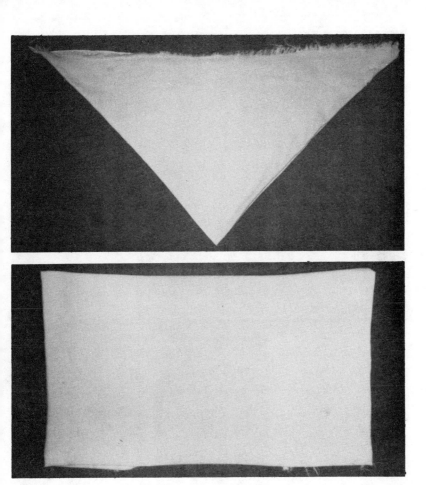

A white textile bag could be folded in two different ways to make
a diaper for the baby of the house. The diapers were washed after
each use and used over and over. This bag will sell for $10 to $12.

The lady's red blouse in this ensemble was made from one 100 pound white textile feed bag that was dyed red. The matching lady's long skirt was made from two 100 pound print, cotton textile feed bags. This ensemble is in excellent condition and will sell for $50 to $52.

Three 100 pound cotton, print textile feed bags were used to make this multicolored dress for a lady. This dress belonged to my mother. Simplicity pattern number 2326 may have been used when making the dress. The dress is in excellent condition and will sell for $20 to $22.

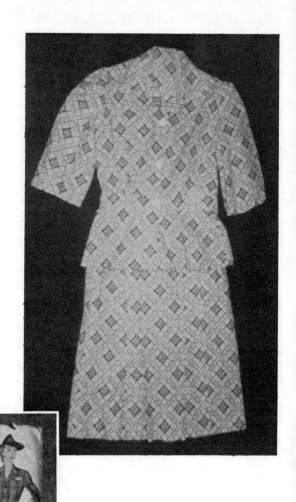

This lady's two piece dress was made from three 100 pound print feed bags. Simplicity pattern number 4385 may have been used. This pattern cost 25¢ when new. This two piece green and red print dress with hand worked buttonholes will sell for $28 to $32.

This lady's dress was made from three 100 pound print feed sacks. This blue and yellow print dress may have been made using DuBarry pattern number 5090 that was printed in 1940 and sold for 15¢ when new. This dress, with a pearl belt buckle and hand worked buttonholes, belonged to my mother. This dress will sell for $26 to $28.

It took three 100 pound print textile feed bags to make this two-piece lady's dress. DuBarry pattern number 5577 may have been used. This pattern cost 15¢ when new. The colors in this dress are deep and brilliant green. Black buttons trim the dress. This dress with hand worked buttonholes, will sell for $24 to $26.

This purple print lady's dress took three 100 pound print feed textile bags to make. Simplicity pattern 2961 may have been used. The pattern cost 25¢ when new. This dress, with pearl buttons and belt buckle, belonged to my mother. This dress will sell for $28 to $34.

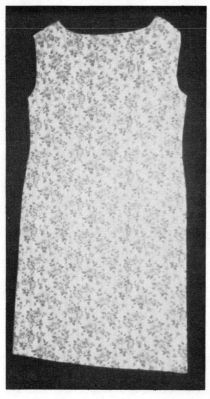

This lady's dress took two 100 pound feed bags for construction. The dress has blue stripes and flowers. This dress was purchased at an antique shop in the Ozarks. It will sell for $20 to $22.

The natural color material from one 100 pound feed sack was used to make this lady's blouse. The blouse has hand worked buttonholes and is in excellent condition. The blouse will sell for $10 to $15.

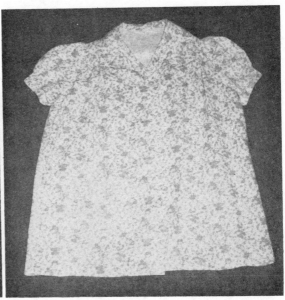

This lady's maternity top was made with fabric from two 100 pound print feed bags. DuBarry pattern number 2404B may have been used. The pattern cost 10¢ when new. This top, with pearl buttons and hand worked buttonholes, will sell for $20 to $22.

This housecoat for a lady was made from two 100 pound print feed bags. The housecoat is white with purple flowers and green leaves. The buttonholes have been hand worked. Simplicity pattern 4214 may have been used when the housecoat was made. This item is in excellent condition and will sell for $16 to $18.

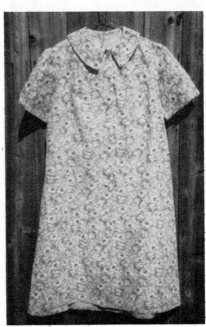

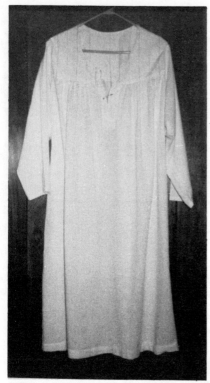

This lady's gown took three 100 pound white textile bags to make. The gown is in excellent condition and will sell for $16 to $18.

This garment could be used as a lady's slip or gown. It was made with two 100 pound white cotton textile bags. This slip would sell for $12 to $14.

These matching mother and daughter skirts were made from the fabric of four print cotton textile bags. These bright printed skirts have red rickrack added. The small skirt will sell for $20 to $22. The large skirt will sell for $30 to $32.

It took one 100 pound print textile bag to make this two-piece bathing suit. McCall's pattern 8736 may have been used when making this bathing suit. This bathing suit is in good condition and will sell for $20 to $22.

This slip and panties for a lady were made from the white cotton textile bags. Lace was added to give a dainty look. These will sell for $10 to $12 each.

Both pair of panties were made from the white cotton textile bags. They both had hemmed legs with elastic in the waist. These panties were made for a lady and will sell for $10 to $12.

Aprons made from the textile print bags are one of the easier items to be found today. Most housewives of this period would wear an apron. There were aprons from the small dainty Sunday apron to the big, cover-up, everyday aprons. The pictures show only a small sample of the many aprons made.

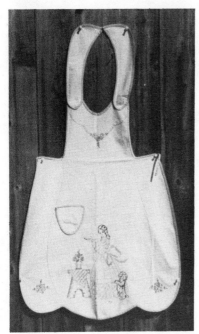

This white apron was made from a white textile bag. An embroidery design and yellow trim has been added. This apron measures 40x23 inches and will sell for $10 to $15.

This cover-up apron was made from a print textile bag. It buttoned in the back. Large ruffles were added over the shoulders. It measures 44x64 inches and will sell for $10 to $12.

This small white apron was made from a white textile bag. A flower pot pocket has been added. This apron measures 22x29 inches and will sell for $8 to $10.

These two everyday aprons were both made from print textile bags. Trim has been added to both. They each measure 38x28 inches and will sell for $10 to $15.

Both these ruffle trimmed aprons were made from print textile bags. These 42x30 inch aprons will sell for $10 to $15 each.

This small apron was made from a print textile bag. Blue rickrack has been added. One of the two patterns, Butterick 4167 or McCall's, may have been used when making this apron. The apron measures 16x26 inches and will sell for $8 to $10.

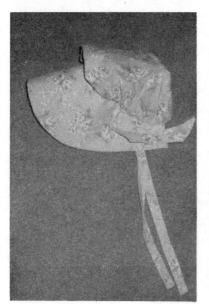 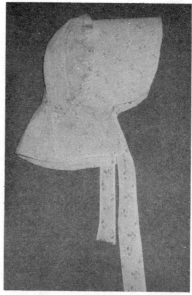

These two bonnets were made from either print flour or feed bags. There are many styles of bonnets that were made during this time. To make the brim of the bonnet stiff, the housewife would cold starch the brim. Each of these bonnets would sell for $12 to $14.

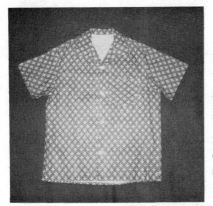

It took two 100 pound print cotton feed bags to make this man's green printed shirt with hand worked buttonholes and pearl buttons. Simplicity pattern 2049 may have been used. The pattern cost 25¢ when new. This man's shirt will sell for $18 to $20.

Men's

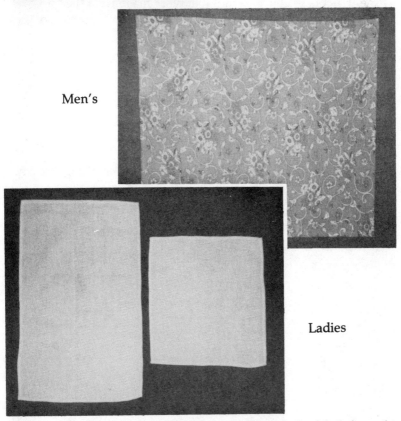

Ladies

Men's and ladies' handkerchiefs were made with the fabric from the white and print bags. The print man's handkerchief measures 19x17 inches and will sell for $4 to $6. The two white ladies' handkerchiefs measure 15x9 inches and 10x9 inches. These will sell for $4 to $6.

This lady's purse and matching hat were made from the fabric of a print textile bag. The print hat has been lined with blue. Each of these will sell for $12 to $14.

This child's drawstring purse was made from fabric from a textile bag. The blue flowered purse has been trimmed in red. This purse will sell for $6 to $8.

Some of the most colorful wardrobes and delightful, cozy home decor was created during the heyday of the textile bags. To help the housewife with fashions and home decor, the National Cotton Council published the following pamphlets: "Sew Easy with Cotton Bags and McCall's Patterns," "Cinderella Fashions From Cotton Bags" and "Bag Magic for Home Sewing." In the "Bag Magic" pamphlet, information on the approximate amount of material in various size bags was given plus directions for removing the printing from bags. This booklet also included patterns and told how many bags would be needed for each fashion. Many of the textile bags were reused out of necessity, but many times the textile bags were used for the appealing look of the print with which the textile bags were made.

Many of the items of apparel that were made of the cotton print and white textile bags can still be worn today. When buying items of apparel that were made of the cotton print and white textile bags, there are two sure ways of identifying the material as bag fabric. Look for the little holes left where the bag was originally stitched with the coarse twine thread. These holes are usually visible washing after washing. Also, look for printing still on the item made from the bags. If the bag had printing directly on it, it sometimes takes many washings to remove all visible lettering.

Many of the items that were made from textile bags were used up and thrown away years ago. So when you do find wearing apparel made from the sack fabric, consider it a very good find.

# CHAPTER 9

# HOUSEHOLD ITEMS MADE FROM THE TEXTILE BAGS

The wonderful smell of brown, crusty loaves of bread baking in the oven of the wood cooking stove filled the weather beaten frame farm house. This house as well as most others across rural America had a feeling of cosiness when a visitor stepped inside. This feeling of cosiness, warmth and comfort came from the stiffly starched ruffled curtains hanging at the windows, the white cotton embroidered tablecloth on the table, the ruffled chair cushions, the carefully pieced and hand quilted quilts covering the beds, the embroidery doily on the end tables, and the colorful rag rugs on the floor. All of these items had been made from the cotton textile bags that feed and flour came in during the first half of the 1900's. The thrifty housewife, both city and country, of the 1920's, 1930's, 1940's and 1950's used every scrap of these print and white textile bags that held staples for farm and home. These smart, thrifty housewives had just gone through the depression and they knew a thrifty deal when they saw it. Bag manufacturers were aware of this fact and they came up with new ways to sell more cotton textile bags to the penny-wise ladies of the home. Ideas such as ready-to-use pillowcase flour bags, aprons all ready to wear when the sack was empty and Disney characters on the printed bags were just some of the ways used to sell products.

180

The lady of the house decorated her home with the fabric from these cotton textile bags. *Sewing With Cotton Bags* published by the Textile Bag Manufacturers Association of Chicago, Illinois listed 46 attractive and practical things to make from the cotton bags including: aprons, smocks, house dresses, beach coats, combing jackets, pajamas, rompers, children's aprons, sunsuits, middies, mattress covers, card table covers, luncheon sets, tray cloths, jelly strainers, handkerchiefs, table runners, garment covers, laundry bags, shoe cases, broom covers, pot cloths, dish towels, dusters, bedspreads, pillows, curtains, pillow cases, ironing board covers, vanity table covers, crib covers, toast pockets, bibs, stuffed animals, dolls, refrigerator bags, suitcase sets, collar and cuff sets, handbags, yardstick holders, book covers, scrap books, dress form linings, hooked rugs, muffin covers and bean bags.

The following pictures show items for household use made from the white, print and colored cotton textile bags. This is only a sample of the many things that were made from textile bags. The uses were many. There is a price guide for the collector of these items.

This laundry bag for dirty clothes hung in some girl's room years ago. The blue-eyed lady was made of white and blue cotton textile bags. She has appliqued flowers on the pockets and a face that has been embroidered. This unique lady will sell for $30 to $32.

Laundry bags were made with cotton textile bags. This laundry bag was made with a 100 pound print textile bag and measures 28x22 inches. This bag will sell for $8 to $10.

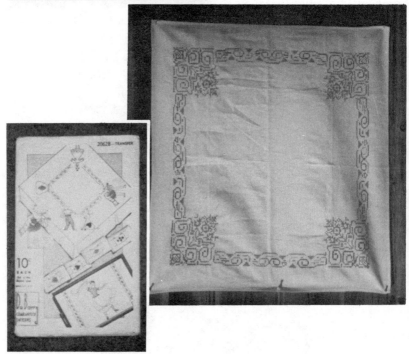

This tablecloth was made with one 100 pound white cotton textile bag. There has been a beautiful embroidery design added to this small tablecloth. Patterns with embroidery designs for tablecloths were sold during this period. The DuBarry pattern 206B that sold for 10¢ when new is an example of patterns used at this time. This 34x32 inch tablecloth will sell for $18 to $20.

This white tablecloth with a yellow border was made with a 100 pound white textile sugar bag. The letters Sugar can still be seen on one side of the tablecloth. An embroidery design and border have been added to the tablecloth. The tablecloth measures 46x46 inches and will sell for $18 to $20.

This small tablecloth was made for a card table with the fabric from a 100 pound textile bag. The tablecloth measures 34x34 inches and has an embroidery design added to one corner. This will sell for $14 to $16.

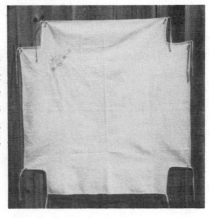

These two dinner napkins were made from a white textile bag. Green trim and a small embroidery design has been added. Each napkin measures 10x10 inches and will sell for $6 to $8.

This set of dish towels (one for each day of the week) was made with 100 pound white feed bags. Each bag was cut in half so it took three and one half 100 pound bags to make the set. Each towel has an embroidery design on it and measures 38x18 inches. The set, including two pot holders and an apron, will sell for $30 to $32.

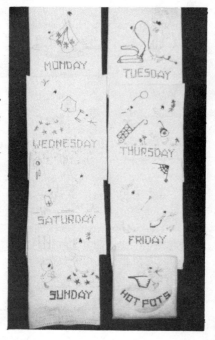

A 100 pound towel bag was used to make the dish towel and two dishcloths. One of the dishcloths still has "Towel Bag" written on it. The dish towel measures 32x18 inches. Each dishcloth measures 18x9 inches. This set will sell for $14 to $16.

Both of these pot holders were made from textile bags. One was made from a white sack and an embroidery design was added. The other was made from a print bag. Each will sell for $8 to $10.

It took two 100 pound print cotton textile bags to make these kitchen curtains. The curtains are 34 inches long and 40 wide. The curtains are in excellent condition and will sell for $12 to $14.

This baby quilt was made with dyed and white cotton textile sacks. The front is made up of 12 blocked pieces joined at the seams by green trim. The material in the blocks have been dyed pink, blue, green and yellow. The quilt has been lined with white textile sacks and quilted. This quilt measures 54x41 inches and was made in 1942. This quilt will sell for $24 to $26.

The center and border of this baby quilt was made with pieces of print textile bags. The quilt measures 36x25 inches. This quilt will sell for $10 to $12.

This sheet was made for a baby bed or crib. It took one and one half 100 pound white cotton textile bags to make. The sheet measures 53x39 inches. This sheet will sell for $10 to $12.

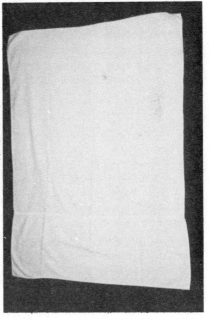

These pillowcases were made from white cotton textile bags. An embroidery design has been added to each 28x18 inch pillowcase. Each pair of pillowcases will sell for $18 to $20.

This pillowcase flour bag is just like it was when the flour was emptied out years ago. The labels or seam has not been removed. This bag measures 28x20 inches. Since this bag is so original, it will sell for $60 to $62.

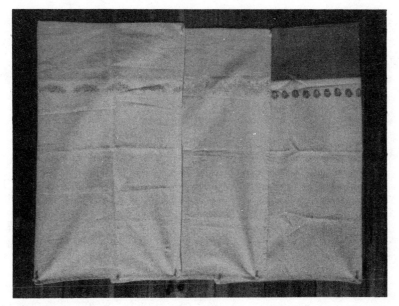

These three pillowcases were all ready-to-use pillowcase flour bags. The holes from the stitching of the flour bag can still be seen on the border of each case. These pillowcases measure 28x17 inches and held 25 pounds of flour at one time. Each pair of pillowcases will sell for $14 to $16.

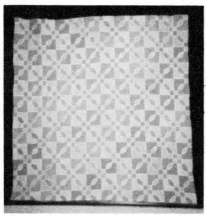

This pink and white quilt top was pieced with white and dyed feed sacks. Lettering can still be seen on the white parts of the top. This quilt top was pieced in the 1940's. It measures 84x82 inches and will sell for $30 to $35.

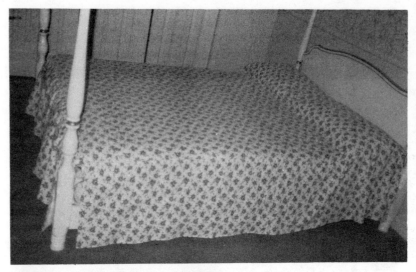

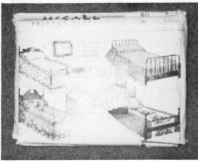

This double size bedspread was made using seven 100 pound print textile bags. The McCall's printed pattern 911 that was copyrighted in 1941 may have been used when making this spread. This bedspread is in excellent condition and will sell for $25 to $30.

This patchwork quilt top was pieced using print and dyed textile bags. Every piece of material large enough to be sewn together was used. This was a popular way of using scraps. The quilt top measures 76x73 inches and will sell for $20 to $25.

This quilt was made with cotton textile bags. The front was pieced with green and pink blocks. The 96x72 inch quilt was lined with white textile bags and quilted. It will sell for $50 to $60.

Picture courtesy of Monnie Cook.

Most of this quilt top was made with print cotton textile bags. The quilt was lined with white cotton textile feed sacks and bound with the same. The quilt was tacked and made in the late 1940's or early 1950's. The quilt measures 89x70 inches and will sell for $50 to $60.

This Windmill quilt was pieced with print and white textile bags. This quilt was pieced in 1945 by Mary A. Wilson, my grandmother. The quilt measures 82x64 inches and will sell for $40 to $50.

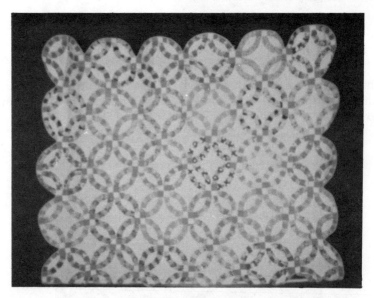

This Double Wedding Ring quilt was pieced mostly with pieces from the print and white textile bags. This was a very popular pattern during the textile bag days. This quilt was made in 1947 by Irene Daniels, my mother. It has been outline quilted. The quilt measures 72x60 inches and will sell for $60 to $75.

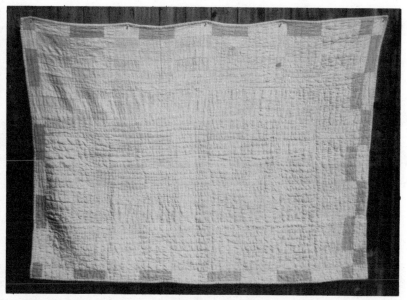

Front

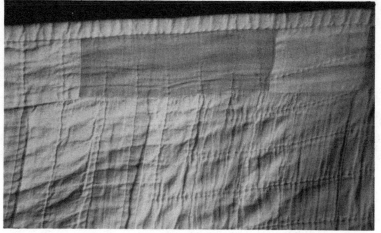

Closeup

The top of this quilt was pieced with tobacco sacks (some dyed, some not). The quilt has been lined with white cotton textile bags. This quilt was pieced in the 1930's by Jan Harrington. The quilt measures 78x56 inches and will sell for $40 to $50.

Picture courtesy of
Jan Harrington

This rag rug was made with pieces torn from the print and colored textile bags. After the pieces were torn into strips, they were sewn together and made into a rug. This hooked rug measures 85x24 inches and will sell for $18 to $20.

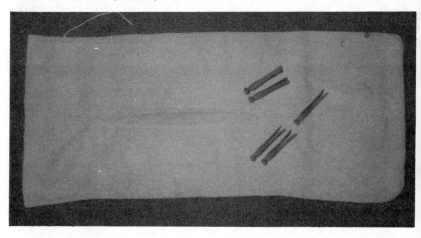

This clothespin bag was made from a bushel size feed bag. The lady had cut a slit in the bag and hemmed it. She would pin the bag to the clothesline and reach through the long slit to get the clothespins as she needed them. The bag measures 35x15 inches and will sell for $8 to $10.

This clothespin apron was made with a print feed or flour bag. The apron measures 16x17 inches and will sell for $12 to $14.

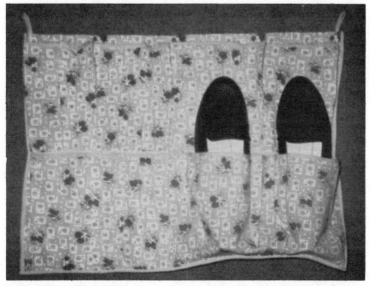

This shoe case was made from a print textile feed or flour bag trimmed in yellow. This case would hold four pairs of shoes. The case would be hung on a wall or closet door. The shoe case measures 21x15 inches and will sell for $14 to $16.

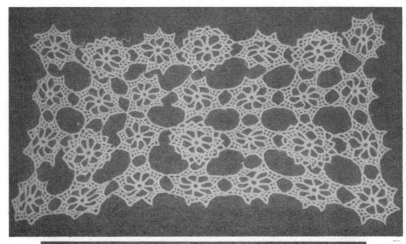

Crocheted, tatted and knitted pieces were made from the twine cotton thread that was unraveled from the seams of textile bags. The pictures show a crocheted scarf for a dresser, edging made for the ends of a dresser scarf and a crocheted piece. These handmade items will sell for $10 to $12 each.      196

The chair cushion and pillow top were made from textile bags. The chair cushion was made with one 100 pound cotton print textile bag. The pillow top was made with a white textile bag and an embroidery design was added. These would sell for $10 to $12.

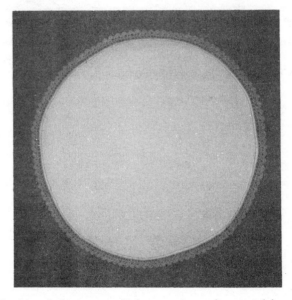

This small white doily was made from a piece of material from a white textile bag. A blue edging has been added. The doily measures 17 inches across. This will sell for $6 to $8.

This table scarf was made from the fabric from a white textile bag. A crocheted edging and a beautiful embroidery design has been added. The scarf measures 32 inches across. This will sell for $10 to $12.

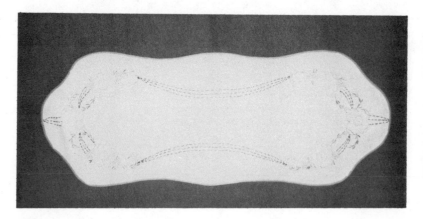

This dresser scarf was made from a white textile bag. A blue edging and an embroidery design has been added. This scarf measures 40x15 inches and will sell for $8 to $10.

This dresser scarf was made from the material of a white coffee textile bag. The words "COFFEE ROASTED & GROUND" are still on the scarf. An edging has been added to the 52x15 inch scarf and will sell for $14 to $16.

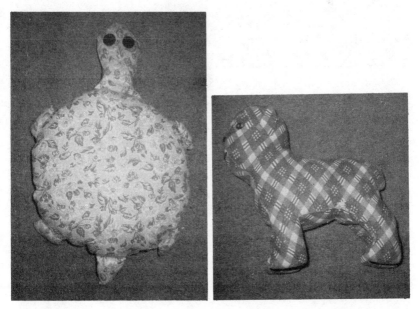

Stuffed toys for children were made with fabric from the print and white textile bags. The dog and turtle were both made with a print textile bag. Each of these stuffed toys will sell for $12 to $14.

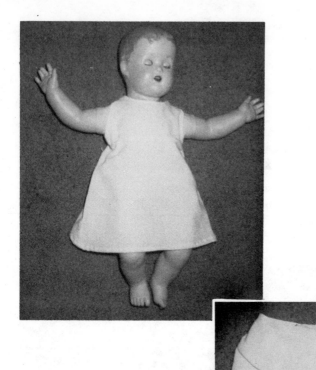

Doll clothes from panties and slips to dresses and jackets were made out of the fabric from the white and print textile bags.

This white slip and panties for a doll were made from a white textile bag. They will sell for $8 to $10 each.

This half slip for a doll was made from a white textile bag. This slip will sell for $10 to $12.

200

Both of these doll dresses were made from textile bags. One was made from white and print textile bags. The other was made with a print bag. These dresses will each sell for $14 to $16.

This print jacket was made for a doll. It was made from a print textile bag. A blue button and pocket were added to the jacket. This jacket will sell for $8 to $10.

When Mrs. America threaded her needle and began to reuse the textile bags, the range of items made was endless. They were limited only by the imagination of the housewife that reused the bags. A complete household could be cleverly and attractively decorated with the intermingling of the print, colored, white and dyed bags. Cotton bags played the primary role in the greatest development in home sewing during this period. Often this material was the shortest and only cut to essential household items.

Laundered flour sacks sold like hot-cakes during the 1940's. They were reused as dish towels and tea towels. Westwood Village Market in Los Angeles, R.H. Macy and Co. of New York and Sears, Roebuck and Co. all sold the laundered flour bags.

Items that were made with the textile bags and are found and bought today, can still be used. Such items as tablecloths, napkins and dish towels are very attractive to use in the home today. The items in this chapter are a sample only, an array of household items made with the textile bags can still be found.

# CHAPTER 10

## BURLAP BAGS

The burlap textile bags are used today and were used even more in the past to package food staples. The burlap bags were never as popular because they could not be reused by the housewife; they were not as clean or as attractive a packaging unit as the cotton bags.

Most burlap bags are made from jute, a bast fiber that comes chiefly from India. The jute plant grows to a height of about 12 feet. It is cut off close to the ground when it is in flower. It is then stripped of its branches and leaves and put through a retting process to loosen the fibers from the stalk. After they are separated from the outer bark, the fibers are dried and cleaned. Because jute is affected by chemical bleaches, it can never be made pure white. Jute is used chiefly for gunny sacks, burlap bags, cordage and binding and backing threads for rugs and carpets. Jute is second only to cotton in the world's production of textile fibers.

Burlap bags were used to package staples like flour, beans, potatoes, seed, feed, produce of all types and many other products. According to a report by the United States Department of Agriculture about 18.2% of the flour packaged in 1931 was packaged in burlap bags. About 3% of the corn meal produced in 1932 was packaged in burlap bags.

One of the main reasons for using the burlap bags over cotton bags was that they were cheaper. The bag manufacturers usually manufactured both cotton and burlap bags. The following pictures and descriptions show a sampling of some of the many burlap bags that were produced. A pricing guide is included for the collector of the burlap bags.

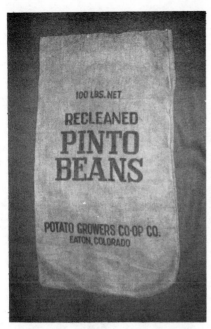

100 pounds of recleaned PINTO BEANS came in this burlap bag. The Potato Growers Co-op Co. of Eaton, CO packed the beans. This is a standard railroad, bean bag guaranteed by Lone Star of Houston. The bag measures 37x21 inches and will sell for $12 to $14.

100 pounds of GOLDEN SPUR POTATOES came in this burlap bag. The potatoes were packed by Hodgell Farms, Inc. of Monte Vista, CO. The bag measures 40x24 inches and will sell for $14 to $16.

100 pounds of SFA FEEDS came in this burlap bag. The feed was manufactured by Cooperative Mills of North Little Rock, AR and distributed by Southern Farmers Association. This bag measures 40x22 inches and will sell for $8 to $10.

100 pounds of NUTRENA FEEDS came in this burlap bag. The feed was manufactured by Nutrena Feed Division of Minneapolis, MN. Langston Bags of Memphis, TN manufactured the bag. The bag measures 40x22 inches and will sell for $6 to $8.

50 pounds of PURINA CHOWS came in this burlap bag. The feed was manufactured by Ralston Purina Company, General Offices, Checkerboard Square, St. Louis 2, MO. The bag measures 36x18 inches and will sell for $10 to $12.

100 pounds of BEACON FEEDS came in this burlap bag. Copyright date on the bag is 1948. Bemis Bag Company manufactured the bag. Beacon Milling Company, Inc. of Cayuga, NY manufactured the feed. The bag measures 39x22 inches and will sell for $14 to $16.

100 pounds of SWIFT'S Cotton-seed Meal Pellets Cake came in this burlap bag. The feed was manufactured by Swift and Company, General Offices, Chicago, IL. The bag measures 39x22 inches and will sell for $8 to $10.

100 pounds of KREY'S Digester Tankage for hogs came in this burlap bag. The tankage was packed by Krey Packing Company of St. Louis U.S.A. The bag measures 40x22 inches and will sell for $8 to $10.

100 pounds of NORTHERN STAR COTTON SEED came in this burlap bag. The cotton seed were mechanically delinted. The seed were Texas state registered. The cotton seed were produced by Wacona Seed Farms of Waco, TX. It states on the bag that these seed were of greater yield, early maturing, and were storm proof. Bemis Bag Co. of Houston manufactured the bag. The bag measures 40x27 inches and will sell for $14 to $16.

COKER'S Pedigreed Seed came in this burlap bag. Coker's Pedigreed Seed, Blood Will Tell, were produced by Coker's Pedigreed Seed Co., David R. Coker, founder, of Hartsville, SC. The bag measures 39x28 inches and will sell for $8 to $10.

50 pounds of KENTUCKY 31 TALL FESCUE came in this burlap bag. The bag was manufactured by the Chase Bag Company of Kansas City, MO. This bag measures 39x20 inches and will sell for $8 to $10.

120 pounds of RICELAND Soybeans came in this burlap bag. The Riceland purity seeds were packed by Riceland Seed Co. of Stuttgart, AR. The bag was manufactured by the Semmes Bag Co. of Memphis, TN. The bag measures 39x22 inches and will sell for $10 to $12.

50 kilos of QUALITY Shelled U.S. Runner PEANUTS came in this burlap bag. Farmers Fertilizer & Milling Company, Inc. of Colquitt, GA produced the peanuts. The bag measures 39x23 inches and will sell for $8 to $10.

GCB COCOA came in this large import burlap bag. The cocoa was produced in Ghana. This bag measures 44x28 inches and will sell for $16 to $18 since it is an import bag.

Burlap bags are used more today than the cotton textile bags. Some products can still be purchased in burlap bags. The burlap bags are usually less desirable as collectibles than the cotton bags are. Very little could be done by the housewife to reuse a burlap bag. Many times the burlap bags were reused by the feed, seed and fertilizer manufacturers. This chapter deals only with a sample of the many, many burlap bags available to the collector. The pricing is for the collector who might wish to begin a collection of burlap bags. The burlap bags are easy to find and are very reasonable.

## BURLAP BAGS NOT PICTURED

100 pound burlap bag that held WIRTHMORE FEEDS. The feed was manufactured by Chas. M. Cox Co. of Boston, MA. The bag measures 40x22 inches ..................................... $12 to $14

100 pound burlap bag that held MASTER MIX HOG FEED. The feed was manufactured by Central Soya, Fort Wayne, IN. The bag measures 39x23 inches ............................ $10 to $12

100 pound burlap bag that held WESTERN POTATOES. The potatoes were packed by E. Miller Farms, Inc. of Antigo, WI. The bag has a picture of a cowboy lassoing a calf. The bag measures 34x22 inches
$14 to $16

100 pound burlap bag that held HOLSUM POTATOES. The potatoes were packed by the Associated Potato Growers, Inc. of Grand Forks, ND. The bag measures 35x24 inches ................. $8 to $10.

100 pound burlap bag that held No. 1, ANTHONY QUALITY, AA Brand, potatoes. The potatoes were packed by Anthony Farms of Scandinavia, WI. The bag measures 34x22 inches ..... $8 to $10.

100 pound burlap bag that held OUR BANNER BRAND PEANUTS. The peanuts were Fancy Hand Picked. The bag measures 37x34 inches .......................................... $8 to $10

Burlap wrapper used to cover bale of cotton during shipping. 106x38 inches, with tags .................................... $12 to $14

# CHAPTER 11

## THE CARE OF TEXTILE BAGS AND
## WHERE TO FIND THE TEXTILE BAGS

Textile bag collecting is new to most collectors and suppliers alike. The lowly feed and flour sacks have hung in some obscure nook or cranny of shops for years. A few would find their way into the scheme of a country kitchen or decor of a country store, but the only real user of the textile bags for the past several years have been the quilt makers.

I have been collecting bags for almost 15 years, and during that time period I have seen the status of the textile bags begin an upward climb. The demand has increased and prices have skyrocketed in some areas of the country. There are very few textile bag collections across the nation.

Textile bag collecting appeals to individuals in different ways. I have seen individuals that collect only the print bags for the array of colors and patterns to choose from. Others collect in only one area such as the sugar bags. Still others collect the items made from the print, white and colored bags such as dresses, shirts, etc. There are some individuals who collect just quilts made from the textile bags. There are many specialty areas within the textile bag collecting field for an individual to choose from.

Man's use of fibers to make clothing and decorative items is as old as civilization itself. Today the collections of textiles include both handmade and machine made fabrics. These documents from our past are not replaceable and every precaution should be taken to preserve the pieces in the best possible manner. The textile bags are finally finding their place into textile collections and museums and not thrown into some dusty barn corner or loft.

The care, display and storage of the textile bag is much like that of any other textile piece. The textile bags are constructed of natural cotton fibers, therefore, they expand and contract, breathe, according to the temperature and moisture content of the air. It has been recommended that cotton textiles be placed in surrounds with a temperature of around 70 degrees Fahrenheit and a humidity level of around 50% relative humidity. Rapid changes in temperature and humidity can cause swelling and shrinking of the fibers and the result is structural damage. Textile bag collections should never be stored in basements or attics where this rapid temperature and humidity change is possible.

Cotton is prone to heat damage and under exposure to excessive heat tends to break down. Cotton is damaged by excessive amounts of light, therefore lighting is very important in the life of cotton textiles. Both visible and ultra-violet light can cause damage. Sunlight is the main source of ultra-violet light and when displaying the bags, either in individual homes or museums, display out of the range of the sun's ultra-violet rays. When home laundering the textile bags, it would be best to dry them in the shade when drying outside. Unbleached cottons show less damage by exposure to sunlight than bleached.

Cotton is vulnerable to action by microorganisms, particularly to mildew. In the home it is well never to store starched cottons since starch fosters the growth of mildew. The cotton textile bags should be stored in dry, airy places. Do not seal textiles in plastics, rather wrap in acid-free paper or muslin and allow the items to breathe.

Some of the textile bags that an individual purchases will need to be cleaned. Wet cleaning, where the bag is cleaned in a water and detergent solution, is usually used. Cotton as a fiber is generally stronger wet than dry therefore it thrives on soap and water washes. The main problem with wet cleaning of the textile bags is the removal of the direct on bag printing. Most of the direct on bag printing was done with wash out inks so they soak out easily.

When washing textile bags or items made from the textile bags, always use caution. Most of the cotton print bags will be color-fast when washed but **always** do a color test to be sure. The bags that have the band and spot labels on them cannot be washed because the paper labels will soak off. Sometimes the spot label can be removed before washing and reglued to the bag after it has been washed. Most band labels are sewn into the bag seam and cannot be removed and reglued after washing. (Remember if the bag doesn't have to be washed – don't.) When washing use a very mild detergent and as little as possible so rinsing will be easier. Always rinse items thoroughly. Textile bags with direct on the bag printing should be watched carefully as it is washed. The ink may start to fade and if it does, take it out at once. (Remember most inks are the wash out kind.) Gently wash bags, never scrub or rub. After washing, rinse well and remove excess water by pressing gently with cotton towels. Lay flat to dry. Large sacks like the cotton pick sack can be washed in the bathtub. Here again, if the sack has printed lettering on it, watch for fading. The lettering is important to the value of a bag so it should be protected if at all possible. The bag may need ironing after laundering. Use a warm iron and protective pressing cloth.

The pictures show what a very gentle, short wet washing can do to restore brightness to a bag.

 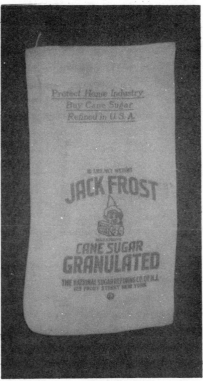

Before       After

Textile bags pop up in unexpected places at times, but some definite places to look for bags will be one of the following: garage and estate sales, flea markets, antique malls and shops, antique shows and sales and auctions.

Garage and estate sales are good possibilities for finding bags and especially good for finding items made from the textile bags. When you buy items or bags from people at garage sales, they can usually give you the history about the item or bag.

Flea markets are an excellent source for textile bags. This has been one of my best places for finding bags.

Antique shops and malls are good places to search for the cotton textile bags. The price will usually be higher than at the flea markets and garage sales.

Antique shows and sales will prove very interesting to the bag collector. Be prepared to pay higher prices for items bought here.

Auctions, both farm and regularly held auctions, are excellent places to look for the textile bags and items made from them. Here the prices paid will vary greatly.

Always be prepared to bargain on prices, especially at flea markets and garage sales.

Bag collecting and the range of items made from the bags will prove to be a fascinating hobby for those who are interested in the textile field. There was such a large number of bags produced that no one will ever complete a collection.

# BIBLIOGRAPHY

Since there are so few books on the subject of textile bags, I have included a list of books, pamphlets and magazine articles on this subject.

## BOOKS

Cowan, Mary L. *Introduction to Textiles*. Appleton-Century-Crofts, Inc. 1962.

*Davison's Textile Blue Book*. N. J. Davison's Publishing Company. 1932, 1942, 1952.

Edgar, William C. *Judson Moss Bemis, Pioneer*. Bellman Company. 1926.

*Flour Brands in the United States and Canada*. Minneapolis. The Miller Publishing Company. 1951.

Kearfott, Clarence B. *Highland Mills*. N.Y. Vantage Press. 1970.

Linton, George E. *Natural and Manmade Fibers*. Duell, Sloan and Pearce. 1966.

Steen, Herman. *Flour Milling in America*. Minneapolis. T.S. Denison and Company, Inc. 1963.

Wingate, Isabel B. *Textile Fabrics and Their Selection*. Prentice-Hall, Inc. 1976.

## PAMPHLETS

*Bag Magic for Home Sewing*. Memphis, Tennessee. National Cotton Council.

*Chase Bagpiper*. Greenwich, CT. Chase Bag Company. Spring, Summer, Winter 1982.

*Cinderella Fashions from Cotton Bags*. Memphis, Tennessee. National Cotton Council.

*Cotton Bags and Bagging*. N.Y. The Cotton Textile Institute. 1927.

*Our First Hundred Years*. Kansas City, Missouri. Percy Kent Bag Company, Inc. 1985.

Ricker, Lacey F. *Feed Bags: Kinds, Cost and Problems*. Washington. U.S. Department of Agriculture. 1954.

*Selling Bemis Cottons for Profit*. St. Louis, MO. Bemis Brother Bag Co. 1959.

*Sew Easy With Cotton Bags and McCall's Patterns*. Memphis, TN. National Cotton Council. 1959.

*Sewing With Cotton Bags*. Chicago, Ill. The Textile Bag Manufacturers Association.

## MAGAZINE ARTICLES

Brackman, Barbara. "Quilts From Feed Sacks." *Quilter's Newsletter Magazine.* October 1985.

Carson, Ruth. "It's in the Bag." *Collier's.* May 4, 1946.

"Fashions in Feed Bags." *American Magazine.* March 1948.

"Feed Bag Fashion." *Woman's Home Companion.* May 1951.

"Foul Rumor." *Time.* March 11, 1946.

"Textile Industry Organizes to Boost Bag Sales." *Business Week.* July 3, 1948.